NEW WAYS IN THEOLOGY

New Ways In Theology

J. SPERNA WEILAND

Translated by
N. D. Smith

GILL AND MACMILLAN   Dublin

First published 1968

GILL AND MACMILLAN LTD.
DUBLIN 1

Cover design by Des Fitzgerald

Printed and bound in the Republic of Ireland by
Hely Thom Limited Dublin

Contents

'The alarming thing is', he said, 'that this time it isn't only the changeable things that are changing, but the unchangeable as well. Anyhow, that's the danger—even for me. Not only dress and manners and bank-balances and the social order, but the sea and the sky—and Westminster Abbey.'

CHARLES MORGAN

Foreword

1966 will go down as a good year in the history of the Church. In the spring, a great meeting was held in the Westfalenhalle at Dortmund which was directed against what is generally known nowadays as the 'new theology'. The battle-cry that brought the 20,000 people who attended this gathering to Dortmund was 'No other Gospel' and this slogan is a direct reference to Galatians 1:6. Anyone who reads this first chapter of Paul's epistle beyond the sixth verse will see that anathema is pronounced in verse nine: 'If anyone is preaching to you a gospel contrary to that which you received, let him be accursed.' *Anathema sit.*

A meeting like the one that took place in Dortmund has not yet been held in the Netherlands, but I am assured that it could still happen. In the meantime, there is a great deal of plain speaking. It has, for example, been said that people like Bultmann, Robinson, Paul van Buren and Dorothee Sölle may perhaps be acting in good faith, but that they are giving stones for bread and are the instruments of Satan, who uses their books—teachings of the Antichrist (1 *John* 4:3)—to lead men astray.

In this situation, there is reason to ask, what is this new theology? (In this context, I am thinking of the work of Paul Tillich, Rudolf Bultmann, Dietrich Bonhoeffer, John A. T. Robinson, Paul van Buren, Carl Michalson, Gibson Winter, Harvey E. Cox, Dorothee Sölle and many others.) In this book, an attempt is made to give as good a description

xi

as possible of this new theology and to show what these theologians have really said and why they have followed their particular course and not a different one. After doing this, I shall not be able to decide whether Bultmann and the rest are really instruments of Satan or not—for this, I should require an insight into faith which very few men possess. It is, however, possible to find out whether many of the criticisms that are heard about the new theology, such as 'the humanization of faith and the anthropologization of theology', really cut any ice and are strictly relevant once we have established at least what 'humanization of faith' really means.

I have therefore tried to provide a description, a survey, an exposition of the new theology and, in so doing, have remained myself, if not completely absent, then at least very much in the background, like the producer of a play. It would certainly have been possible—and indeed I had every occasion—to put in a word myself here and there, but I felt that it was most important to allow these theologians to speak as much as possible themselves. In this way, the reader will be able to see for himself whether their teaching contains anything that seems to him to be pure heresy or not. What is more, not only had these theologians, in my opinion, to be given the chance to speak for themselves—they had also to be allowed to do so in their own terminology. Expressions like Paul Tillich's 'ultimate concern', Bultmann's *Existenzialinterpretation* and so on could therefore not be avoided. I have, however, elucidated them when they are introduced for the first time. I hope that, in this way, these theologians' own works will be made more accessible. That is my main purpose in writing this book.

At the same time, the book had to be kept within the limits that our present impatient age demands as far as books are concerned. Many things had to be said very briefly and sometimes not even said, but simply fleetingly indicated. I have had to do this throughout the whole book, but especially in the case of classic Roman Catholic or

Protestant theology. Here, I have had to confine myself to brief references, trusting that everyone knows that Amsterdam itself is much bigger than the signpost pointing to it, and that the structures themselves are far more complicated and contain more light and shadow than my brief outlines of them. My presentation of the new theology is also rather schematic, although perhaps less so than that of established theology. It undoubtedly requires further elaboration. Tillich, Bultmann, Bonhoeffer and others will be dealt with separately and consequently in greater detail in a series of theological monographs, of which this book forms a part, but it was obviously necessary to provide a general survey of the whole field before these individual monographs appeared.

The plan of the book is simple. First, a rough sketch is made of the landscape in which the new theology finds its orientation—a secularized world with a very different 'image of the world' from that of our forefathers. Then the path taken by the modern reconnoitrers is followed, and what will emerge from this is that there is no single new theology but rather a series of projects which are, at some points, even mutually contradictory—in other words, that Tillich is different from Bultmann, that Bultmann is different from Bonhoeffer, and so on. Finally, an attempt is made to find out what the beginning of a new map looks like.

This book, then, does not provide a complete survey of the new theology. The work of, for example, Heinrich Ott, Karl Barth's successor in Basle, is not discussed. There is another, even more serious omission. Although an impressive *aggiornamento* is taking place in the Roman Catholic Church and Catholic theology is undergoing a far-reaching renewal which no episcopal pronouncements, aimed at putting the Catholic house in order, can divert from its course, I have neither the space in this book nor the intimate knowledge of Henri de Lubac, Yves Congar, Karl Rahner and many others, to include them. I feel partly justified in this omission as a book on precisely this subject is due to appear shortly.

The fact that Karl Barth is only mentioned occasionally requires some explanation, in view of his essential part in the great renewal of Protestant theology in the twentieth century—it was indeed Barth, and Barth alone, who began this great movement with his *Epistle to the Romans*. But once again, I lacked the space and several excellent reviews of his theology have already appeared. Moreover, there will probably be a book about him in this series. Also, with a slight alteration to the text, it is possible to say of Karl Barth what Ludwig Feuerbach said in the nineteenth century of Hegel: 'He belongs to the Old Testament of the New Philosophy'. But I must hasten to add what Kierkegaard said of Hegel in the nineteenth century: 'Hegel is a great thinker—no one would deny him that, even if it were not proclaimed with fanfares' or what Heidegger said of him in the twentieth century: 'Since Hegel, everything, not only in Germany, but in the whole of Europe, is simply counter-movement'.

In writing this book, I have taken into account the possibility that there may well be study groups in parishes, universities and elsewhere, consisting of people who wish to extend and deepen their knowledge and understanding of the new theology, or individuals who want to do this on their own. With this in mind, I have commenced each chapter with a short bibliographical review which may point the way to further reading. For obvious reasons no Dutch bibliography has been included in this English version. I have tried to find books and articles that are easily obtainable, but have not always succeeded. I can, however, guarantee that anyone who aims to increase his knowledge and appreciation of the new theology will do so if he reads the books mentioned in the bibliographies.

Is the new theology—I do not attach any importance to the name—really new? Or is it no more than a new variation of the old game? There is, of course, a continuity with the tradition of the Church, which is present in the work of all these theologians, although most clearly in the case of Paul Tillich. At the same time, there is also a break with the past that is, moreover, connected with what is usually known, in German circles, as the 'liberal theology'. What is the situation really? In *Encounter*, December 1965, Dom Aelred Graham wrote, in connection with the Second Vatican Council, that the conciliar discussions and even the interventions on the part of theologians such as Hans Küng, Karl Rahner and Henri de Lubac—he made an exception in the case of Yves Congar—were no more than 'a debate between the members of a closed circle of mandarins within the agreed terms of their system'. Is the new Protestant theology really new? I believe that it must be said that a new theological experiment is really taking place here, although this is not happening without continuity with tradition, and that this experiment is concerned with 'the secular meaning of the gospel'. It is beginning to look as though we are no longer agreed about the system and the method and as if the 'agreed system' no longer holds. 'But then it is high time for us to go to Dortmund . . .'

There will, of course, be people who are not happy about the fact that the author of a book is himself absent from that book. He must therefore appear on the stage for a moment to say that he has faith in the play that is about to begin and that he does not believe everything that it contains, but that he knows that, for a number of people of all kinds, the new theology is a way that can be followed 'with glad and generous hearts' (*Acts* 2:46). And now the time has come for him to disappear again, with the words of Kierkegaard: 'If anyone were polite enough to assume that I have an opinion and if he were, in his politeness, prepared to go so far as to adopt that opinion because it was mine, then I should be sorry that his politeness should be extended to someone who was unworthy of it and that his opinion should be no different from mine'. Let the play begin . . .

Amstelveen, 4 September 1966.

The Landscape

Secularization

BIBLIOGRAPHY

AN enormous number of books have been written in recent years by sociologists, psychologists, theologians and philosophers about secularization. Only the most important theological works dealing with this problem are listed in this bibliography.

A good introduction to the subject will be found in articles under the titles 'Säkularisation', 'Säkularismus', etc. in encyclopedias such as *Religion in Geschichte und Gegenwart*—the most important being those on *Säkularismus* written by C. H. Ratschow and J. C. Hoekendijk—and in the *Evangelisches Kirchenlexikon*. Further reference can also be made to the *New Catholic Encyclopedia*, New York, 1967, and to the *Encyclopedia of Philosophy*, New York, 1967.

The work of Friedrich Gogarten is still fundamental and the essence of what he has to say will be found in his book *Verhängnis und Hoffnung der Neuzeit, Die Säkularisierung als theologisches Problem*, published in 1953 by Friedrich Vorwerk in Stuttgart. A cheap edition of this book appeared in 1966 in the series *Siebenstern-Taschenbücher* (no. 72), published by the Siebenstern-Taschenbuch Verlag in Munich. For Gogarten, secularization means, among other things, man's becoming independent as a direct consequence of the gospel and especially of the (re)discovery of the gospel by the Reformers. There is no English translation of *Verhängnis und Hoffnung der Neuzeit*. Anyone wishing to familiarize himself with Gogarten's thesis can, however, also consult his

3

Demythologizing and History, SCM Press, London, 1955.

Two other important books are F. Delekat's *Über den Begriff der Säkularisation*, which appeared in 1958 and is notable for its careful formulations, and M. Stallmann's *Was ist Säkularisierung?*, which was published in 1960 by J. C. B. Mohr in Tübingen in the series, *Sammlung gemein-verständlicher Vorträge*.

The most important Dutch contribution to the study of secularization is, in my opinion, Dr A. T. van Leeuwen's great work, *Christianity in World History*, London, 1964. The secularization of the modern world began, according to Dr van Leeuwen, with the breakthrough of the 'autocratic' cultures of the ancient world in the Old Testament. I must also mention Professor C.A. van Peursen's article, 'Man and Reality, The History of Human Thought', *The Student World LVI*, 1963, in which secularization is described as the transition from an ontological to a functional way of thinking. Harvey E. Cox acknowledges his debt to this article in his *The Secular City*.

A book that was published in 1965 by Chr. Kaiser Verlag in Munich should also be mentioned. This is *Säkularisation. Von der wahren Voraussetzung und der angeblichen Gottlosigkeit der Wissenschaft* by Professor A. E. Loen who is, in this book, particularly concerned with the problem of secularization in the sciences, one of which is theology. Loen rejects the secularization in theology in the works of Paul Tillich, Rudolf Bultmann, Dietrich Bonhoeffer and John A. T. Robinson, because secularization, in his view, means adapting ourselves to the pattern of this present world (*Rom.* 12:2).

Little can be found about secularization in Paul Tillich and Rudolf Bultmann, but Tillich's opposition to what he called 'supranaturalism' and Bultmann's 'demythologization' of the New Testament are closely related to secularization. It is quite different in the case of Dietrich Bonhoeffer: although the word secularization does not occur at all in his *Letters and Papers from Prison*, this book, published by the SCM Press, London, in 1967 (an American translation of the original German work, entitled *Prisoner for God*, was published by Macmillan of New York in 1954), forms one of the most important documents of theological speculation about secularization, which the author described as the development which led to modern, 'religionless' man's 'coming of age' (*Mündigkeit*) in the twentieth century. An important commentary on these letters and thus, indirectly, a contribution to the discussion about secularization is G. Ebeling's essay, 'Die nicht-religiöse Interpretation biblischer Begriffe', in *Die mündige Welt*, Vol. II, Chr. Kaiser Verlag, Munich, 1956, pp. 12-73.

Secularization is discussed in detail in the works of John A. T. Robinson and in the new American theology. John Robinson's most important work in this connection is his contribution, 'The Debate Continues', in *The Honest to God Debate*, SCM Press, London, 1963. Among the American theologians, Gibson Winter has taken the secularized world especially into account as the landscape in which theology has to find its orientation. His most important book in this respect is *The New Creation as Metropolis*, published by Macmillan of New York in 1963—the second chapter especially should be read. It is not difficult to recognize Gogarten's influence on Winter's views.

A FEW HISTORICAL NOTES

THE word 'secularization' is, of course, derived from the Latin *saeculum*. The origin of the word is obscure—it was possibly Etruscan. Its earliest meaning is unknown. In classical Latin, it meant a period, and especially a century (cf. French *siècle*). Ancient Rome celebrated its *ludi saeculares*—festivals marking the end of an old century and the beginning of a new one. The word *saeculum* did not have an unfavourable meaning in classical Latin.

It was, however, used in a different sense in the Vulgate, the Latin translation of the Bible, to render the Greek *kosmos* (world) or *aion* (period, age), thus signifying the

tension between this world in which we live and the world—
not a different world, but this world differently!—to which
God calls us, the tension between darkness and the light.
In this way, there is reference in one of the parables (*Matt.
13:22*) to the *sollicitudo saeculi*, the 'care of the world', which
estranges man from God and from life. In the Vulgate,
saeculum is seen as playing opposite God in the cosmic drama
in which man is at stake. Thus Paul spoke in 1 Corinthians
1:20-31 of the wisdom of God, contrasting this with the
wisdom 'of the world', of this century or *saeculum*, and
warned us, in Romans 12:2, not to conform to this world or
saeculum. In 2 Timothy 4:9, we are told that Demas, *diligens
hoc saeculum*, 'in love with this world', has left Paul, and
because of his love of this world has separated himself from
God and gone to Thessalonica like the prodigal son in the
parable. *Saeculum* is therefore a dialectical concept—it is
God's world, his creation, but at the same time it is also the
world without God, the world of high-handed authority, of
alienation, sin and death.

The medieval antithesis between *saeculum* and *religio*, the
saecularis and the *religiosus*, developed from these data.
'Religion' was the world of the religious, of monks in their
monasteries, and *saeculum* was the profane world surrounding
them. In the general hierarchy—even in matters of faith,
medieval thought was always hierarchical—the religious
were placed above those believers who spent their lives in
the world. Although these two worlds were more or less
completely separate, it was possible for a man to move from
one to the other. A religious could be 'secularized', that
is he could transfer from the religious to the secular, worldly
state.

Frequently, however, the word secularization had quite a
different meaning—that of the expropriation of Church
property, such as lands or buildings. One of the consequences
of the Reformation was an extensive 'secularization' of
ecclesiastical possessions—the Church was, in other words,
dispossessed of much of her property. Further secularizations

took place after the Peace of Westphalia, which marked the end of the Thirty Years War in Germany and at the same time of the war between the Netherlands and Spain, and during the French Revolution—'tous les biens ecclésiastiques sont à la disposition de la nation'—and during the rule of Napoleon.

The word secularization has also acquired another and much wider meaning—so wide in fact that it has become almost meaningless. In the Middle Ages, there was, as we have seen, a sacral world and a profane world, *religio* and *saeculum*. The 'secular' world—the state, politics, science, philosophy and so on—had to comply with religion, which, in concrete terms, meant the Church. From the late Middle Ages onwards, there was increasing opposition to the Church's claims to power and this resulted in the gradual secularization of politics, science and so on. In a struggle that lasted centuries, a struggle marked by violence, disregard for truth and many scandals, but basically a struggle for freedom, the authority of the Church was slowly weakened and autonomy was gradually established. The most important events in this long struggle were the Renaissance, the Reformation with its rejection of the medieval dualism of *religio* and *saeculum*, and the Enlightenment.

WHAT IS SECULARIZATION?

In the official account of a discussion held in September 1959 at the Château de Bossey on 'The Meaning of the Secular'—the report was written by Charles West—secularization was defined as 'the withdrawal of spheres of life and thought from religious and ultimately also from metaphysical control and a living in these spheres in terms of what they are in themselves'. Secularization is thus the end of a world in which the Church has the last word in all spheres of life. The unity of this world is no longer known to us. Our world is in fact a number of different worlds which are autonomous and unrelated to each other.

In the case, for example, of a scientific hypothesis, there is no necessity in a secularized world to ask whether such a hypothesis is in conflict with the teaching of the Church or not. (We have only to think, in this connection, of the Church's struggle in the past against Copernicus and Galileo and for the Ptolomaic idea of the universe, or of the controversy during the nineteenth century about Darwin and his *On the Origin of Species*.) All that is necessary now is to ascertain whether a hypothesis can be verified and applied within the framework of science itself. Science is no longer dependent on the Church's approval or disapproval. We can therefore say that science has become autonomous or that it has become secularized. We can also say, with Bonhoeffer, that man has reached the end of a very long path in European history and has at last come of age. But, if we use Bonhoeffer's term *Mündigkeit*, 'coming of age', we should not forget that he himself did not use it in a sociological or a socio-psychological context, but within the framework of man's social and historical development. Man's factual immaturity, the fact that he has not yet come of age—the 'radar' inner-directed type of David Riesmann—is not in conflict with his historical coming of age as Bonhoeffer defined it.

Having outlined this aspect of secularization—the fact that science, politics and so on have become independent and that religion and metaphysics no longer control the whole of life—does not, however, mean that everything that needs to be said about this phenomenon has now been said. Secularization also refers to a fundamental change in man's experience of being in the world. If we look back at history, we can without difficulty see that, in the past, man was convinced that life on this earth was not the real life, that it was not Reality. As Hymn No. 75 of the hymn book of the Dutch Reformed Church puts it, 'It is not here below'. Besides and above this world, there was another Reality, the true, metaphysical Reality. That was the reason why Nietzsche called Christianity Platonism for the people— Plato saw, above our changing, transient world, the world of eternal Ideas, the world of Being and taught that our world could exist only if and insofar as it participated in this other real world. If we consider twentieth-century man's understanding of—and insight into—himself and his world, and his way of expressing himself in philosophy and literature, we are bound to conclude that this other, true, metaphysical Reality is no longer present for him and that he has learnt to live on earth as Marx wanted him to live—*enttäuscht*, that is, having come to a proper understanding of himself. *Enttäuscht*, in the Marxist sense, does not mean (or at least, it does not only mean) that we just have to make the best of things as they are in a spirit of resignation. It means primarily that we have seen through a *Täuschung*, a delusion or fallacy, and have left it behind forever.

In *The Secular City*, Harvey E. Cox similarly characterizes the style of secular society with the words 'pragmatism' and 'profanity'. Pragmatism is modern man's practice of dealing, in the most matter-of-fact way possible, with the problems that arise, without letting himself be confused by religious and metaphysical considerations. Cox regards John Kennedy's procedure as the outstanding example of pragmatism. Profanity is defined by Cox as living within the confines of this earth and without any supraterrestrial reality imposing itself on us.

In this situation, then, it is possible to describe secularization as a liberation—man is free to live his own life and to be responsible for himself. There is no authority to lay down to me what I have to do and what I must not do. I must decide for myself and accept the responsibility of my decision. In the whole complex event of secularization, this is the element that has appealed most strongly to Friedrich Gogarten and Gibson Winter and even to Harvey E. Cox. For the first time in history, man has been placed in a situation of historical responsibility which is not rejected by any 'god' or in the name of any sacral reality and taken out of his hands. Cox himself has said that the world has become man's task and man's responsibility.

STAGES IN HISTORY

We must, however, dig a little deeper if we are to reach the essential meaning of secularization. Dorothee Sölle says, in her book *Stellvertretung,* that our situation is characterized by 'the loss of a definite manner of thinking and speaking'. Her words are very reminiscent of Heidegger's about the end of metaphysics—it is no longer possible for us to experience and speak about being as it was experienced and discussed in ancient times. On the way towards language—the title of one of Heidegger's last works (*Unterwegs zur Sprache*)—we must begin anew. We are at the beginning of a new age in history.

In the nineteenth century, the great theoretician of positivism, Auguste Comte, distinguished three stages in the history of man. Man, Comte said, had begun in the religious or mythological stage, had passed through the metaphysical stage and had now finally reached the positive stage of his development. Professor C. A. van Peursen's 'model' is similar to Comte's—there are three stages in the history of human thought, the mythological, the ontological and the functional. Harvey E. Cox makes use of van Peursen's model in *The Secular City,* at the same time linking to each of the three stages in human thought a stage in the history of human relationships. The mythological way of thinking was, according to Cox, found in primitive society, the ontological in the state (the *polis*) and finally functional thought is found in the 'technopolis'. Elaborating his theory, Cox goes on to say that the transition from the first to the second stage took place in ancient Greece. This transition is illustrated, in Cox's view, in Sophocles' drama, in which the *polis* and primitive society are opposed to each other in the figures of Creon and Antigone. The victory of Creon over Antigone represents the victory of the *polis* with its law and order over the primitive social relationships and at the same time that of ontological thought over mythological.

Twentieth-century man is also living in a period of transition: from the second to the third stage. The growth of technology and socio-economic organization has brought about a new society which is breaking down the frontiers between states and causing them to disappear. This laborious transition from the *polis* to the new structures of human society coincides with the disappearance of ontological thought— or of metaphysics, to use Heidegger's word—and the emergence of a new, functional way of thinking. Cox's 'model'— and we should not forget that it is no more than a model, and thus a highly simplified representation of reality!—is of importance to our theme of secularization because, within the framework of this model, secularization can be described as the transition from the second to the third stage in the history of man.

But what, then, is ontological thought and what is functional thought? Van Peursen defines ontological thought as 'the analysis of the "what" of things', as the answer to man's question about the being, the nature, the essence of things. 'What is it?'—that is the question which ontological thought answers with its definitions. What is man, what is the world, what is love, truth and justice and who or what is God? In ontological thinking, the threat is always present that things will become debased into 'things in themselves', which can be defined without a moment's thought being given to the relationships in which they are placed and act on each other. Ontological thought defines the limits of things, distinguishes them and maps out the hierarchical order of being. It says 'what it is'—God, man, reason, the world, 'things in themselves'.

Functional thought, on the other hand, does not ask about the 'what' of things, but how something works. 'According to a functional way of thinking, reality is there in its functioning, in other words, something shows its reality in doing, in acting.' Thus functional thinking does not ask who God is, but what he does and how he works in reality, in our terrestrial history. 'The Name is not a doctrine, but a power that overcomes the human reality, but in history, not as a metaphysical control.'

I must conclude with these brief notes and refer the reader to the texts of van Peursen and Harvey Cox themselves, in the hope that it will at least have become clear that this transition to a functional way of thinking—and that is, after all, what secularization is, according to this view—also has enormous consequences for theology. The whole style of theological thought has changed and the opportunities of mutual misunderstanding have increased.

This is, moreover, not the last word about secularization, and the model may be too crude for us to be able to work with it. Be that as it may, we must always distinguish a number of different elements in the event 'secularization'. We have already noted that science, politics and so on have become independent and have been withdrawn from the sacral order that embraced the whole of life, and that this has been experienced as a liberation of man so that he can now live his own life and be responsible for himself. We no longer have one single scheme at our disposal, to which we can orientate ourselves—Denis de Rougemont's *commune mesure*—but we live with a number of frequently contradictory orientations. We are no longer conscious of eternal truths and values above us—like fixed stars. Furthermore, 'a definite manner of thinking and speaking' is no longer possible for us.

However secularization may be defined by individual thinkers, there is a general conviction that we are living on a dividing line in history. John A. T. Robinson regards our present age as that of a new reformation. Harvey E. Cox goes even further. In his opinion, it can only be compared with the period at which the ancient world of the myth declined and history began.

SECULARIZATION AND CHRISTIAN FAITH

THE most obvious way in which the Churches could respond to secularization would be to reject it and combat it. Secularization can easily be described as a falling away from the God of the Trinity—with all the consequences of this falling away—and the struggle against secularization as a resistance of the Devil himself. If this view is taken of the situation, secularization and Christian faith are implacably opposed to each other and Christians are clearly called to take part in a twentieth-century crusade against the secular world. This militant attitude was undoubtedly the rule before 1940 and it was not exceptional after 1945. The great encyclical, *Humani Generis*, which appeared in 1951, was one of the many documents of this crusade mentality, which was directed against Marxism, 'historicism', existentialism and the 'new theology'.

One of the first people to find his way towards a different appreciation of secularization was Dietrich Bonhoeffer. In 1944, he wrote in one of his letters, 'Roman Catholic and Protestant historians agree that it is in this development that the great defection from God, from Christ, is to be seen; and the more they claim and play off God and Christ against it, the more the development considers itself to be anti-Christian.'[1] His thought acted as a breakthrough in this unanimity of Catholic and Protestant historians (and theologians!)— the development that has led to modern man's 'coming of age' was seen as not in itself anti-Christian, but the attacks of Christian apologetics had made it so. We must simply realize that there is a new situation in which the gospel must be proclaimed to the world and we must begin by accepting this situation 'from God's hand'. But Bonhoeffer went even farther—not only have we to accept this new situation more or less reluctantly perhaps, but we must also see with gratitude that secularization—and here it should be pointed out once again that the word 'secularization' does not occur in Bonhoeffer's writings—frees us from the 'religious' misinterpretations of the gospel that are as old as the Church herself. Then Bonhoeffer went on to provide a religionless interpretation of the Bible, which is discussed later in this book.

This interpretation of the history of the last few centuries

[1] *Letters and Papers from Prison*, London 1967, 178.

met with a considerable response. Like Bonhoeffer, John A. T. Robinson's point of departure is that secularization, this change in man's way of experiencing himself and his world and this revolt against the patterns of thought inherited from a pre-scientific age, must not be combated, but must be accepted as 'a neutral fact'. In itself, the secular world is no less Christian than the world that we are leaving behind and must leave behind.

Friedrich Gogarten went even farther. For him, secularization is not simply a neutral fact that we must accept if we are not to become estranged from our own age. It is the consequence of the proclamation of the gospel in the European world and, even more than this, a consequence of the Protestant interpretation of the gospel: 'Secularization can be viewed theologically in such a way that it has its basis in the essence of the Christian faith and that it is the legitimate consequence of this.' The gospel, after all, liberates man from the powers that held him captive, makes him historically responsible and takes away the world's divine halo. In 1953, what Gogarten had to say caused a small revolution— secularization was not an anti-Christian phenomenon, as the Churches had always thought and taught, but the legitimate consequence of God's work in history! In order to substantiate his affirmation—an affirmation which also maintains that the whole history of the Church from the late Middle Ages until the twentieth century was based on an enormous misunderstanding in respect of the historical event and the essence of the Christian faith!—Gogarten could point to the fact that secularization had begun in Europe and that it could not have begun anywhere else. He could also have found support for his thesis in modern philosophy—in Heidegger, who attributes the world's indifference to God, and loss of religion to Christianity, and in Karl Jaspers, who has established in his philosophy of history that modern science and technology could not have come about if the 'biblical religion' had not introduced an entirely different experience of being-in-the-world from that of ancient man.

The conditions for science in the modern sense of the word were not present in the ancient world.

Gogarten's interpretation of historical relationships, which is, at the same time, an interpretation of the Christian faith, was taken over by Gibson Winter and elaborated by Harvey E. Cox and by Dr van Leeuwen in his book *Christianity in World History*. These writers say that we should not look for the origins of secularization in the Reformation or even in the New Testament, but that we should go even farther back in time, in fact, to the Old Testament. It is there—in the accounts of the creation, the exodus and the covenant of Sinai—that the secularization of the world was begun and indeed accomplished. The consequences of this dynamite placed under the sacral order have unfolded themselves in the centuries of history that have followed.

Very many questions arise in connection with this view of secularization which cannot be dealt with here. The greatest theological question of our own times, however, is concerned with the relationship between the Christian faith and the experience of reality and patterns of thought of a secularized world. Are we to oppose the latter in the name of faith, or must we begin by accepting them? Is the secularized world revolting against God, or is secularization a 'neutral fact' or even a legitimate consequence of the proclamation of the gospel in the European world? To put it in a simple and rather crude form, there would seem to be two possibilities:

1. We can cling to the 'old' faith even though twentieth-century man says that it means nothing to him, simply because we must remain faithful to what God entrusted to our forefathers and has entrusted to us. Our attitude will be that 'the old-time religion is good enough for me' and for all men. The Churches will undoubtedly go on losing more and more of their members, because there will always be many who will accompany Demas, 'in love with this *saeculum*', on the road to Thessalonica—and it is a wide road!

2. Or we can read the Bible again, in the light of a

secular world's experience of reality, which, whether we like it or not, is our own. 'Our task is not to insist on a definite interpretation that has been given to us, but to insist on the never-ending interpretation of the gospel' (G. Ebeling). If there really is a new situation, then the living tradition of the same gospel will speak to us differently from the way in which it spoke to our fathers.

Despite all the differences that there are between the various projects for a new theology—and these differences are certainly very great—there is absolute unanimity in the choice of the second possibility as the only possibility. This does not mean that the gospel should be adapted to a secular world's experience of reality and that this experience of reality should have the last word in respect of what we can still believe and of what we cannot believe any longer. It means that the proclamation of the gospel should be disso- ciated from an outdated way of thinking and from an out- dated idea of the world.

SECULARIZATION AND SECULARISM

THE acceptance of secularization and the rejection of a ghetto mentality and a crusading ideology is accompanied in the new theology by a resistance to secularism. This distinction between secularization and secularism can already be found in Gogarten. If secularization is the liberation of man, making him historically responsible in an open world, secularism is the totalitarian arrangement of the world into an easily surveyed whole in which there can no longer be any question of asking or of not knowing, but in which all asking and not knowing simply disappears. Secularism there- fore means either nihilism, in which there is no more asking because no answer is given, or a totalitarian ideology, which presents itself as the way of salvation and in which not knowing has disappeared. It is the great task of faith to keep the world to its authentic secularity and to prevent it from going off the rails into secularism.

Gogarten's ideas about secularization and secularism recur in the works of Carl Michalson and Gibson Winter. But Winter stresses far more than Gogarten the need for a secularization of the Churches, which still retain their patriarchal character, impose their authority on men, and thus refuse to accept the ultimate consequences of secularization. In connection with the debasement of genuine secularization to the level of secularism, he maintains that the Churches can also become secularist in their insistence on having the last word, their proclamation of eternal truths and their fundamentalist and dogmatic claims to know how things are. A secular faith and hierarchical authority are mutually exclusive. The Church of the future must therefore be different from the Church of the past. This question will be discussed later on in this book.

A Changed Image of the World

BIBLIOGRAPHY

COUNTLESS books have been written about the changes that have taken place in our image of the world during the last few centuries.

There is not much to be found in modern philosophy about these changes in themselves, but far more about the impossibility of devising an image of the world in which the whole of reality is taken into account. In his *Philosophie*, published by the Springer Verlag of Berlin in 1931-2, Karl Jaspers, in a terminology that is frequently reminiscent of that of Kant, argued that science was an orientation in the world, but that the whole of reality (the 'world') was in fact beyond the range of the sciences. What we can expect of science is not an image of the world, but an orientation in the world (*Weltorientierung*). In addition to his *Philosophie*, I should also mention Jaspers's much shorter work, *Vernunft und Widervernunft in unserer Zeit*, which was published by R. Piper of Munich in 1950. In this book, Jaspers demonstrated that true science has been forsaken in the 'total knowledge' (*Totalwissen*) of Marxism and psycho-analysis. Apart from the works of Jaspers, those of Martin Heidegger are very important. One of his essays is especially interesting in this connection. This is *The Age of the World-view*, which was originally written by Heidegger in 1938, but was not published until 1950. The published version included a number of important additions and was translated by M. Grane. This American translation appeared in *Measure* in 1951, pp. 269-84. In his

18

rather inaccessible terminology, Heidegger argued in this essay that technology was the ultimate consequence of the totalitarian organization of the world into an 'image' in European metaphysics.

Rudolf Bultmann especially has devoted attention to the consequences in the sphere of faith and theology of the changed image of the world. The contrasts between the ancient and the modern image of the world have, in Bultmann's view, made 'demythologization' necessary for us. The relationships between the modern image of the world and faith, or, in this case, theology, were discussed by Bultmann in his essay, *The New Testament and Mythology*, which appeared in the collection *Kerygma and Myth*, translated by R. H. Fuller and published by Harper of New York in 1961, and in dialogue with Karl Jaspers in *Die Frage der Entmythologisierung*, which was published by R. Piper of Munich in the collection *Kerygma und Mythos III* in 1954. In the other projects of a new theology as well, there is naturally a close connection between the changes in the image of the world and a new understanding of the gospel.

NON-FIGURATIVE THOUGHT

THE world, orientation in the world and our image of the world have already been briefly discussed in this book and we have established that the world has become a number of disconnected worlds which cannot be viewed as a whole. We have also seen that we no longer have one single scheme at our disposal towards which we can orientate ourselves, but that we have to live with a number of different orientations which are frequently contradictory. Finally, we have shown that a distinction has to be made between the gospel itself and an outdated image of the world. We must now discuss these points in rather more detail.

Perhaps the most telling description of our present situation, with its changed image of the world, has been provided by T. S. Eliot in The Waste Land:

What are the roots that clutch, what branches grow
Out of this stony rubbish? Son of Man,
You cannot say, or guess, for you know only
A heap of broken images, where the sun beats,
The dead tree gives no shelter, the cricket no relief,
And the dry stone no sound of water . . .

We live in a cosmos that has fallen apart, a countryside of broken images, a heap of fragments. My only comment is that, for most of us, this countryside is by no means as desolate as it is for Eliot. We do not live among dead trees in a ravaged landscape without shade from the beating sun, but in a country where we at last feel free and can begin to live, where we have at last been released from our 'casing' (Karl Jaspers's *Gehäuse*).

We may also express the situation thus—thought, which has, up to the present, had a figurative character, has now become non-figurative. The fragments of figurative thought are lying all around us and we have not devised any new image of the world. We are resigned to the fact that the images are broken and that we have to orientate ourselves in the world without being able to view it as a whole. There is science and probably also faith, in which case we may already point to the fact (in anticipation of what follows) that these two orientations are not (necessarily) mutually contradictory.

If we look back at history, we can see that Christianity was figurative. With the information given to it in the Bible, it had a comprehensive view of the world, which embraced God and man, the past and the future, the creation and the last judgement. There were questions which were not always answered. The mind of God was frequently unfathomable. 'Humbly we adore the secrets that are hidden from us'—the words are from the sixteenth century *Confessio Gallica*, the confession of the French Churches, which goes on to tell us that we should worship these mysteries 'without asking above our degree' (sans nous enquérir par dessus nostre mesure).

But, even though there were secrets and questions without answers, nature and history were seen as a whole.

The Enlightenment, that rational interlude in European history, broke with this classical Christianity, but thinking still remained figurative, even though Kant knew more about the unfathomable character of Being than the philosophers who had gone before him. What we know, after all, is not reality in itself (the Kantian *Ding an sich*), but the reality which presents itself to us in space and time and in the categories of our thought. Coming to the nineteenth century, we find Hegel's system of Being, which shows us how Reason unfolds itself in history and how God becomes man, and the Marxist *Totalwissen*, which reproduces the necessary development leading from primitive to classless society. The nineteenth century also gave us historicism and positivism, but in all these systems, thinking remained figurative or, to use van Peursen's word, magical. If we are to believe Karl Jaspers, this is also true of psycho-analysis.

There is, however, a difference between the situation in the nineteenth century and that which prevailed in the preceding centuries. Up to and including the eighteenth century—for the sake of argument, we could say that the year 1789 marked the division—there was only one scheme of orientation, the Christian, a symbiosis of biblical faith and Greek metaphysics. This scheme was accepted without question—it was so self-evident that even the rational philosophers of the Enlightenment, Leibniz, Lessing, Kant and others, were orientated towards it. In the nineteenth century, however, mankind was confronted for the first time in its history with a series of mutually contradictory schemes —the Christian faith in all its different varieties, idealism, materialism, positivism, historicism and Marxism. They were all 'figurations' and they all had a *Totalwissen*, which had still to be amplified and further elaborated, but which formed a fixed framework for all later amplifications and elaborations. Men lived in their Christian, their Marxist or their positivist 'casings' and assailed each other again and again with arguments, which were refuted, but which never really found their mark and still less led to conviction, because they only held good within their own figure of reality. This is, of course, too crude a representation of nineteenth-century thought, a way of thinking that continued far into the twentieth century (although the courage, the imagination, the lively mobility and the tendency to carry argument to the ultimate consequences which also characterized the thinking of the nineteenth century were absent in that of the first half of the twentieth), but it does enable us to see that an entirely new situation had arisen—one of mutually contradictory schemes of orientation within one world.

What, then, is this different situation of the latter half of the twentieth century, since, shall we say, 1945? The landscape is one where we 'know only a heap of broken images', where we live amid the ruins of images of the world. As Ernst Haeckel said, we can no longer see through the puzzle of the world. 'Then I saw all the work of God, that man cannot find out the work that is done under the sun ... Even though a wise man claims to know, he cannot find it out' (*Eccles*. 8:17). The wise man may perhaps be wiser. Anyone who 'claims to know' is, whatever else he may be, certainly not a wise man. The demolition workers are pulling down every house. The Marxists are looking for a 'dialectic without dogma' (R. Havemann). Scientists are more aware of the limits of science and observe them more carefully than they did in the nineteenth century. Twentieth-century philosophy is orientation in the world and the 'illumination' of existence (Karl Jaspers), a waiting for Being to speak and for the divine God (Martin Heidegger) or ultimately a metaphysics of silence (Ludwig Wittgenstein). We are situated in history and we are unable to gain a view of the whole.

A similar development from figurative to non-figurative thinking has also taken place in the natural sciences. Classical physics was figurative—it had an image of reality which, although it still required amplification, was nonetheless firmly established in broad outline. But in works such as *Physik und Philosophie,* a book published in 1959 in the series Ullstein Bücher, Frankfurt a. M., Werner Heisenberg has shown that modern physics no longer has an image of the unknowable reality, the 'in itself' of reality: 'Physics does not describe and certainly does not explain nature as it is in itself. Rather, it is a part of the interaction between nature and ourselves and describes nature as subjected to our questioning and to our methods.' There is no longer any question of explaining. Modern physics explains nothing, it describes, and even here a reservation has to be made: 'The quantum theory no longer permits nature to be described objectively.'

This also is rather too crude a scheme, but it may serve to throw some light on the twentieth-century manner of thinking. In this landscape, the Christian faith and theology also take on a very different character, and this was one of the most important reasons for the *aggiornamento* in the Roman Catholic and in the Protestant churches. Faith has become an orientation in history. It is not an orientation towards the conscience, a Christian moral system or the eternal truths of the Christian faith, but an orientation towards the tradition of salvation that has been given to us in the Old and New Testaments, an orientation which cannot be made to conform to a single image of reality. Theology today justifies this orientation. This is what Paul van Buren, for example, meant when he borrowed the term 'blik' from the English philosopher R. M. Hare to describe faith. This 'blik' is a historical perspective that is decisive to the whole of life, but it does not give us a single image of the world. And there are many things that we do not know.

IMAGE OF THE WORLD AND CHRISTIAN FAITH

In this situation, is it not absurd to give as much thought as Rudolf Bultmann has done to the implications contained in the modern image of the world for the Christian faith? It certainly seems so. In his discussion with Bultmann about the demythologization of the New Testament (see bibliography), Karl Jaspers began by saying that Bultmann was mistaken in appealing to the modern image of the world. 'The most important characteristic of modern science is that it does not put forward an image of the world, because it realizes that this is impossible. For the first time in history, it has set us free from all images of the world . . . It knows its limits . . . It knows that it does not know Being itself, but things in the world.' Jaspers was right in his characterization of modern science, but he had not in fact put his finger on the matter with which Bultmann was concerned, so Bultmann replied: 'I do not think that modern science provides an image of the world in the sense in which Jaspers understands the word.' But, though we live without an image of the world, we do live under the influence of modern science and technology and this means that things that could be believed by men living in biblical times can no longer be believed by men today. Such things are indeed not only incredible, but also impossible. Even though modern science may not provide an image of the world, it does give a model of reality which has a far-reaching effect on our lives.

The model is one of a closed reality with an uninterrupted sequence of cause and effect. When Bultmann refers to a closed reality, he means that, in this model of reality, a possible intervention by transcendental powers—angels, demons, the devil or God—in the order of nature and history is not taken into account. That is the methodical atheism of modern science and we live, in this sense, atheistically. We do not expect any miracles which will break this sequence of cause and effect (a relationship which is often only partly visible to us). We have no faith in God's possible intervention if things get beyond our control. As Harvey E. Cox has said, the world has become man's task and man's responsibility.

The model was quite different in the ancient world. Not only could miracles happen—they did happen. And not only could God intervene in the world—he did intervene. Men were possessed by evil spirits, Herod was struck down by an angel of the Lord because he refused to honour God (*Acts* 12:23) and so on. Unlike the world of today with its closed reality, the world of biblical times was open. Is faith a return to that open world or is it something else?

It is, of course, possible to say that Bultmann did not make the happiest choice of terminology in this context and that the word 'closed' in particular suggests a kind of enclosure that Bultmann himself did not intend. At the same time, however, it is possible to recognize that this is one of the essential questions confronting the Christian faith in the modern world—must we cling to a model of reality that is no longer our own and drag it along with us or is there another course open to us? The new theology insists that there is another course, which we must, in fact, take, and that the credibility of the gospel in the twentieth century is at stake here.

Philosophy

BIBLIOGRAPHY

THE not always cordial debate with philosophy is as old as theology itself. Throughout the centuries, philosophy has been one of the features of the landscape through which theology has been passing and, indeed, not simply a feature of the landscape, but a travelling companion. In our own times, philosophy means especially phenomenology and existentialism on the continent, and logical positivism and linguistic analysis in England and America. The dialogue with Marxism has as yet hardly begun.

I. M. Bochenski has provided a good survey of modern philosophy, discussing such movements as phenomenology, existentialism, neo-positivism and neo-realism, in his book *Contemporary European Philosophy*, which was published by the University of California Press, Berkeley, in 1959. Wittgenstein's *Philosophical Investigations* and his linguistic analysis are, however, not discussed in Bochenski's fairly detailed work.

There are many good books about existentialist philosophy (Karl Jaspers, Gabriel Marcel and others) and about phenomenology (Martin Heidegger, Jean-Paul Sartre, Maurice Merleau-Ponty and others). H. Spiegelberg's *The Phenomenological Movement, a Historical Introduction*, published in two parts by M. Nijhoff in The Hague in 1959, for example, provides a detailed survey. A great deal has been written about Martin Heidegger, but there is no relatively simple introduction to his thought, and his own works are

26

almost unreadable for anyone who has not patiently familiarized himself with Heidegger's idiom.

Two of the works of Ludwig Wittgenstein, who is representative of the most recent developments in English philosophy, have been published in editions in which the German text and an English translation appear in the same volume. The first is L. Wittgenstein, *Philosophische Untersuchungen—Philosophical Investigations*, translated by G. E. M. Anscombe, Oxford, 2nd. edn., 1958. The second is L. Wittgenstein, *Logisch-philosophische Abhandlung*, with a new translation by D. F. Pears and B. F. McGuinness and with an introduction by Bertrand Russell, London, 3rd impression, 1966. This book is published in the series International Library of Philosophy and Scientific Method. Paul van Buren (*The Secular Meaning of the Gospel*, pp. 85-101) and Ian T. Ramsey ('Contemporary Philosophy and the Christian Faith', *Religious Studies*, Vol. 1, Number 1, pp. 47-61) both have something to say about the significance and implications for theology of contemporary English philosophy.

To claim that a sound knowledge of the philosophy of our own times is necessary if we are to follow the new theology would be to claim too much. But a great deal that is contained in the new theology would inevitably remain obscure to those who are not familiar with philosophy, although this depends very much on the theologian in question. Bonhoeffer's thought, for example, can be followed without knowing modern philosophy, but Bultmann's existential interpretation of the New Testament would certainly be quickly misunderstood if his work were read without any knowledge of Heidegger's *Sein und Zeit*.

It was above all existentialism which first set theology on a new course. Kierkegaard, that solitary precursor of existential philosophy in the nineteenth century, was the first and, after him, came Heidegger, who is generally (and incorrectly) included among the existentialists. It is to existentialism that theology owes its renewed insight into faith as a 'total act of the whole man' and not as a mere acceptance as true of what the Church teaches or of what is said in the Bible. In addition to this statement of Emil Brunner's, there is also Paul Tillich's observation that the philosophy of existence must be regarded as 'the good luck of Christian theology', because it has led us back to the Christian view of humanity. A great deal, therefore, can be found in Tillich's anthropology that has been taken from existentialism and especially from Heidegger. Bultmann's work is quite simply unthinkable without Heidegger, to whom he dedicated his first collection of essays in 1932. The influence of existentialism is also very great in American theology, and especially in that of Carl Michalson.

What is remarkable is that Karl Jaspers is not often mentioned in modern theology. Yet Jaspers has devoted more attention than any other modern philosopher to the relationship between philosophy and Christian faith. He regards the religion of the Bible as of inestimable importance to our civilization and has said that 'we philosophize from the biblical religion'. But his philosophy has had very little noticeable effect on theology, although an exception must be made in the case of the Swiss theologian, Fritz Buri. Theology has not been influenced by Jaspers, but by Heidegger—by his description of the structures of humanity, such as care, anxiety, 'being to death' and so on in *Sein und Zeit,* and by his notes on the end of metaphysics in his later works.

This is what the existentialists, the phenomenologists and the contemporary English philosophers have in common— they have all said farewell to metaphysics. The new theology is in accordance with modern philosophy in its anti-metaphysical character. But what does the word 'metaphysics' mean, a word that is so often used in the new theology, often so scornfully and always without being defined? In his essay 'Nietzsches Wort: Gott ist tot', which is included in the collection *Holzwege* (published by Vittorio Klostermann, Frankfurt a. M. in 1950), Heidegger says that metaphysics is not a doctrine and not a part of philosophy, but the *Grund-*

gefüge, the basic framework or plan of being which underlies all the rest and which distinguishes a supraterrestrial reality from a terrestrial and which takes as its point of departure the fact that this supraterrestrial reality bears up and determines the terrestrial reality.[1] The situation is somewhat different in the 'Viennese circle' and in neo-positivism, where metaphysics has to do with everything that transcends the limits of experience. For the Viennese circle and the neo-positivists, metaphysical statements are those statements which can neither be contradicted nor confirmed and which cannot be verified and are therefore simply 'nonsensical', nonsensical in this context being identical with unverifiable. Bidding farewell to the supraterrestrial reality—God, the ideas, the moral law and so on—and confining themselves to the limits of experience, modern philosophers are looking for a new and strict and matter-of-fact objectivity. As the phenomenologists express it, our attention should be turned 'to the matters themselves', or, according to the English philosophers, there should be silence when the limits of experience have been reached.

Bidding farewell to metaphysics is, in the case of Heidegger, at the same time a farewell to the image of the world and to the Christian faith. This may perhaps be connected with his own Roman Catholic past, but that alone does not account for it. Christianity and metaphysics were, for him, an indissoluble unity. He wrote about this in a remarkable and almost unnoticed fragment in his little book *Identität und Differenz*. Referring to scholasticism, in which the subject of discussion, in a profound game of thinking, was God as the first cause (*prima causa*) and at the same time his own cause (*causa sui*), Heidegger said, 'Man cannot pray to this God, nor can he sacrifice to him. Man cannot kneel in reverence before the *Causa sui*, nor can he dance and make music before

---

[1]In Heidegger's own words, we have, in metaphysics, to think of 'das Grundgefüge des Seienden im Ganzen, sofern dieses in eine sinnliche und übersinnliche Welt unterschieden und jene von dieser getragen und bestimmt wird'.

this God. God-less thinking, that must remain aloof from the God of philosophy, from God as *causa sui*, may therefore be closer to the divine God, which means here that it may be more free for him.' In this sense, Heidegger's thought is atheistically on the way to the divine God. It is moreover not impossible that Wittgenstein's metaphysics of silence may linger in the vicinity (in silence) of the divine God.

These notes about the relationship between philosophy and the new theology are, of course, not complete. Much more remains to be said. But I have tried to do no more than suggest the landscape through which the new theology is passing—a secularized world, full of broken images of the world and inhabited by atheists who, like all men, are inclined to all evil and to all good.

The Reconnoitrers

Paul Tillich

BIBLIOGRAPHY

THE most important work that Paul Tillich wrote in the course of his long life (1887-1965) is the three part *Systematic Theology*. Two editions of it have appeared—one, American, published by the University of Chicago Press, Chicago (I, 1951; II, 1957; III, 1963), and the other, English, published by Nisbet & Co., London (I, 1953; II, 1958; III, 1964). These two editions are, unfortunately, differently paginated.

A much shorter work, which will be found more suitable as an introduction to Tillich's thought, is *Biblical Religion and the Search for Ultimate Reality*, of which there are also two editions: one, American, published by the University of Chicago Press in 1955, and the other, English, published by Nisbet & Co. in 1956. A cheap edition of this book was brought out by the American publisher in the series Phoenix Books (no. 154).

A somewhat earlier book, which will also provide a very suitable introduction to Tillich's ideas, is *The Courage to Be*, published by the Yale University Press, New Haven in 1952. This book provides a very good picture of Tillich's dialogue with existentialism (especially Heidegger) and of the basic intention of his thought.

Whereas Tillich was concerned in *The Courage to Be* with the 'existentialist' theme of courage and fear and with the doctrine of God, he showed in *The Dynamics of Faith* what belief is. This book was published in 1957 by Harper &

33

4

Brothers, New York, who also published, in 1958, a cheap edition in the series Torchbooks (no. 42).

Tillich himself regarded and described the course of his life and thought up to the time of his emigration to America in 1933 as a series of 'frontier situations'. With a number of well-selected fragments from Tillich's works, this outline of his life is included in *Auf der Grenze. Aus dem Lebenswerk Paul Tillichs*, Evangelisches Verlagswerk, Stuttgart, 1962. A cheap edition of this book was brought out in 1964 by the Siebenstern Taschenbuch Verlag.

Although the fundamental tendency of his thought is less clearly expressed in his sermons than in his strictly theological works, these can certainly also provide access to Tillich's theology. The earliest collection of his sermons, *The Shaking of the Foundations*, was published in 1948 by Scribner's Sons in New York. Another English edition was published in 1949 by the SCM Press of London. (John A. T. Robinson quotes frequently from this collection of sermons in his *Honest to God*.) The same publishers brought out, in 1955 and 1956 the collection, *The New Being*.

For the sake of completeness, I should mention that the Evangelisches Verlagswerk has been publishing, since 1959, Tillich's *Gesammelte Werke*, in which Tillich's earlier works, such as his writings on religious socialism, are included. These collected works will comprise twelve volumes. So far, seven volumes have appeared.

A good introductory vindication of the *Systematic Theology* has been given by Alexander J. McKelway in *The Systematic Theology of Paul Tillich. A Review and Analysis*, Lutterworth Press, London, 1964. Karl Barth's *Church Dogmatics* is behind the questions that McKelway has written in the margin of the *Systematic Theology*. H. Zahrnt devotes pp. 382-467 of his book, *Die Sache mit Gott. Die protestantische Theologie im 20. Jahrhundert*, published by Piper of Munich in 1966, to Tillich. Finally, I should mention a collection of studies, edited by Kegley and Bretall, *The Theology of Paul Tillich*, Macmillan, 1964.

A special characteristic of these three volumes [Tillich is referring here to the three volumes of his *Systematic Theology*], much noticed and often criticized, is the kind of language used in them and the way in which it is used. It deviates from the ordinary use of biblical language in systematic theology—that is, to support particular assertions with appropriate biblical quotations. Not even the more satisfactory method of building a theological system on the foundation of a historical-critical 'biblical theology' is directly applied, although its influence is present in every part of the system. Instead, philosophical and psychological concepts are preferred, and references to sociological and scientific theories often appear. This procedure seems more suitable for a systematic theology which tries to speak understandably to a large group of educated people . . . for whom traditional language has become irrelevant. Of course, I am not unaware of the danger that in this way the substance of the Christian message may be lost. Nevertheless, this danger must be risked, and once one has realized this, one must proceed in this direction. Dangers are not always a reason for avoiding a serious demand. It sometimes appears in these days that the Roman Catholic church is more open to the demand for reformation than are the churches of the Reformation. Certainly, these three books would not have been written if I had not been convinced that the event in which Christianity was born has central significance for all mankind . . . But the way in which this event can be understood and received changes with changing conditions in all periods of history. On the other hand, this work would not have come into existence either, if I had not tried during the larger part of my life to penetrate the meaning of the Christian symbols, which have become increasingly problematic within the cultural context of our time. Since the split between a faith unacceptable to culture and a culture unacceptable to faith was not possible for me, the only alternative was to attempt to interpret the symbols of faith through expressions of our own culture. The result of this attempt is the three volumes of *Systematic Theology*.[1]

These words from the foreword to *Systematic Theology III* (which appeared when Tillich himself was almost eighty!) are reminiscent of the work of Schleiermacher, that great nineteenth-century theologian, whose supreme anxiety was that faith and society (science) would become estranged from each other, that Christianity and 'barbarism', science and disbelief, would become identical. That possibility is again present, or rather, it is still with us and it is clear from the fragment quoted above that Tillich accepted the literary heritage of Schleiermacher in his own situation. Is it possible to believe and at the same time to live fully in the twentieth century and in its society and civilization, without the one standing in the way of the other? This is a question which is met with, in different formulas, in Rudolf Bultmann, Dietrich Bonhoeffer, John A. T. Robinson, Paul van Buren and many others—in fact, in the whole of the 'new theology'.

All around us are people who already know the answer— Christians who maintain that twentieth-century civilization is a renegade civilization that we must, in faith, combat (as 'a civilization rejected by faith') and unbelievers who, when they think of Christianity (regarding it as 'a faith rejected by civilization'), think of Nietzsche's hermit, who had not yet realized that God was dead. And all around us too there are people 'for whom traditional language has become irrelevant' and who still do not want to or cannot give up their faith, because

He has driven a nail through my hand

M. Nijhoff.

It was for these people that Tillich wrote his *Systematic Theology*.

[1] P. Tillich, *Systematic Theology*, *III*, London 1964, 4–5.

I have referred to the nineteenth-century 'father of the Church' and I could also have referred to Dr K. H. Roessingh and his characterization of modern theology: 'Modern theology is an attempt to make eternal peace between Christianity and scientific civilization, and, what is more, between Christianity and the scientific civilization that had been determined by the intellectual life of the eighteenth century.' Eternal peace—that was rather an exaggerated claim. Scientific civilization is, after all, not a timeless factor, but is historically conditioned—it was different in the Middle Ages from what it had been in the ancient world and it is again different in the present century from what it was in the nineteenth. But modern theology has certainly been concerned with the question of making peace between faith and modern civilization, faith and science, and modern theology is, in many respects, the link joining Schleiermacher and Tillich.

Paul Tillich was born in 1887 in the little village of Starzeddel, which is now in East Germany. He was the son of a Lutheran minister. He studied theology and philosophy, first in Berlin, then in Halle and Tübingen, and abandoned the confessional faith of his childhood years. In 1914, he became a chaplain in the German army and his experiences in the First World War were decisive for his later development. He read not only the Bible—especially the prophets—but also Marx and Nietzsche. He discovered that the Church and her language were not reaching most of the men entrusted to his care. He made decisions. As a socialist—and that really meant something in those days—he returned to Berlin in 1918 and became one of the leading spokesmen for religious socialism and the editor of the *Blätter für religiösen Sozialismus* (1920-24). In 1924 and 1925, he was a professor at Marburg, where he met Rudolf Bultmann and Martin Heidegger. Heidegger was at this time working on his *Sein und Zeit I*, which was published in 1927. This work had a deep influence on both Tillich and Bultmann. Between 1925 and 1929, he was Professor of Philosophy at Dresden, a post which he held also at Frankfurt a. M. from 1929 until 1933, in succession to Max Scheler. It was at Frankfurt that he wrote his book, *Die sozialistische Entscheidung*, one of the first basic criticisms of emergent national socialism. It was immediately withdrawn and 'pulped' when Hitler came to power. In the meantime, he began, in his lectures on dogmatism, to put the first touches to what was later to become the *Systematic Theology*. In 1933, he was removed from his post and, like so many others in Nazi Germany, he went to America. From that moment onwards he disappeared from the European scene and it was not until some time after the Second World War that his voice was heard again in Europe. He was associated with the Union Theological Seminary of New York from 1933 until 1955 and after 1955 he was a professor at Harvard. He was almost eighty years of age when he died in the summer of 1965.

IN DIALOGUE WITH TRADITION

ACCORDING to Karl Jaspers, philosophy is only possible in dialogue with others—with tradition. Tillich could have said the same about theology. The whole history of philosophy and theology can be found in his *Systematic Theology*. The indices will help the reader to trace those thinkers who guided Tillich on his way, but they will not tell him everything, since Tillich frequently does not say whom he has consulted in his deliberations, whether in agreement or in disagreement with their views. It is a remarkable fact, for example, that, in that part of the *Systematic Theology* in which he discusses fear, he does not mention Kierkegaard at all and mentions Heidegger only once, and then in passing.

The man who dominates Tillich's thought is Luther. At first sight, this is not so clear, but on closer consideration the *Systematic Theology* can be seen to bear a decidedly Lutheran stamp. The 'Protestant principle' that is so fundamental to Tillich's theology (and to which I shall be returning later) is a variant of Luther's *sola gratia*, 'by grace alone'. But, in addition to Luther, we must also mention at once the man whom we have mentioned already—Schleiermacher, the man who, within the framework of German idealism, tried to reconcile the religious tradition with modern thought and whose feeling of absolute dependence returns in Tillich as a knowledge of and a search for an ultimate, all-embracing and meaningful Reality. There are also clear traces of mysticism in Tillich's thought, and Karl Barth, whose theology was so firmly opposed to mysticism, also influenced Tillich and provided various elements for the great edifice of the *Systematic Theology*. What is perhaps even more remarkable is that, although Tillich was decidedly Lutheran in his thought, Roman Catholic thinking was not foreign to him. Not only do Teilhard de Chardin and the new Catholic theology come within his horizon, but also Augustine and even scholasticism, which is nowadays so much maligned, and the great scholastic theologian, Thomas Aquinas. We may well wonder whether a writer's inclusion of ideas and elements drawn from so many varied and even mutually contradictory traditions does not bear witness to a highly unmanageable way of thinking and it is certainly astonishing that the thinking that has in fact emerged from these very different elements has such a strange and logical consistency.

Then there are the philosophical schools and the individual philosophers who have contributed to Tillich's thought: German idealism, Hegel and especially Schelling, to whom Tillich long ago dedicated his first study, and the great opponents of idealism in the nineteenth century, Kierkegaard, Karl Marx and Nietzsche, and also the philosophy of life and existentialism, especially Heidegger, and then even ancient philosophy—Aristotle and above all Plato, of whom A. N. Whitehead has said that the whole of Western philosophy is no more than a series of footnotes on his unforgettable dialogues. It would also be possible to approach and interpret Tillich's thought from that vantage point—as a series of existentialist and theological footnotes on Plato, the philosopher of the Eros and of the imperishable metaphysical longing that makes man transcend all his other questions and ask about what is one and good and real, about 'ultimate reality'.

Tillich is all this, but he is above all himself—a thinker of the twentieth century who, seized by the gospel, set himself the task of expressing the truth of faith in such a way that it could be understood by those many people 'for whom traditional language has become irrelevant' and understood as an answer to the questions that they put, to the question that they themselves are!

THEOLOGY AS A DIALOGUE

ONE possible way of constructing a dogmatic theology is to take the Bible and the tradition of one's Church as one's point of departure and then to endeavour to formulate the *kerygma*, the proclamation of the message as it comes to us in the Bible, in such a manner that a kerygmatic theology emerges. In Paul Tillich's view, it was and is to the great merit of both Luther and Karl Barth that, listening to the word, as it spoke to them in the Bible, they both provided a kerygmatic theology of this type. (In Barth's case, Tillich was thinking here, not of the *Church Dogmatics,* but of the *Epistle to the Romans.*) Such kerygmatic events are the very lifeblood of theology, but they do contain two great dangers for theology. The first of these dangers is that the kerygmatic theology can easily lead to a fundamentalist attitude—'it is in the Bible' and so that is how it is and what is said in Scripture must be believed exactly as it is said in Scripture. The second is that this type of theology may perhaps no longer speak directly to men but go over their heads and that the truth will no longer have its 'feet on the ground' because it ceases to provide an answer to men's questions and to elucidate their situation.

For this reason, Tillich took a different starting-point and began with man. Let us, he said, begin by listening to the people of our own times before we address them. Let us find out what they say about themselves, their own situation, their being in the world. Let us discover their insight into, their understanding of themselves. When we have done that, we shall perhaps be able to interpret the kerygma in such a way that it relates to men in their contemporary situation. And then another theology will take its place beside the kerygmatic theology—say, an apologetics theology.

Listening to the people of our own times means consulting psychology, sociology and anthropology, observing how people express their views about themselves in modern literature, in poetry and drama and in the visual arts—I am reminded here of a fine essay by Tillich on Picasso's Guernica—and above all becoming orientated in the philosophy of the twentiety century. For Tillich, this was existentialism and especially Heidegger, and not logical positivism and 'linguistic analysis'.

From this study it emerges that man is a being who asks and, in asking, transcends himself. He asks about reality, about a life without 'ambiguity', about the courage to be. He would not ask if he were not estranged from reality and aware of his estrangement. But he would not be able to ask if he were not connected with the reality that he has forsaken and lost in his estrangement. His situation is the one expressed in such an unforgettable way by Augustine in his Confessions: 'Our hearts are restless until they have found their rest in thee'.

That is, among all the 'concerns' that man still has—because he is a being who does not find his own identity, but is on the way towards himself and who also has what he is as his task, a being who is not yet finished and will never be finished—his ultimate and deepest 'concern'. To this it must also be added, in a terminology that is more reminiscent of Bonhoeffer than of Tillich, that the reality which is sought in this ultimate and deepest 'concern' cannot be found outside the world, but only in it and in devotion to the penultimate 'concern'.

This question can, of course, be set on one side and people can resign themselves to the facts that this is life and that things are as they are, and carry on until they can carry on no longer. But the question still remains and they still go on waiting for something that has no name and is more real than anything that we can give a name to. The whole of history is full of references to man's search for himself, for reality, for the life that is truly Life, for the Spirit who makes all things new. 'It is the question of a reality in which the self-estrangement of our existence is overcome, a reality of reconciliation and reunion, meaning and hope.'[1]

That is the question. And it is the task of theology, in interpreting the symbols of the Christian faith, to answer this question, because the kerygma is the answer to this question. It speaks, after all, about the New Being, about the new creation of 2 Corinthians 5:17, which renews the life of men, about the power which makes not only the lives of individuals, but also the life of a human community, new. The question is not a question without an answer.

The method of the *Systematic Theology*, the method of correlation, is the simple consequence of this original point of departure. First philosophy, then theology; first man and his questions, then God and his answer; never the one without the other. They are not dependent on each other, the question and the answer, philosophy and theology. The answer is not implied in the questions, nor are the questions deduced from the answer. Philosophy is not a secret theology, nor is theology a final rounding off of man's understanding of, or insight into himself. Both are autonomous and independent, but they are both there, and it is the task of the *Systematic Theology* to bring to light the correlation which is already there before theology does anything. In history, man is never without God and God is never without men. 'Systematic theology proceeds in the following way: it makes an analysis of the human situation out of which the existential questions arise and it demonstrates that the symbols used in the Christian message are the answer to these questions.'[2]

[1] *Op. cit., I*, 70.
[2] *Op. cit., I*, 55.

AGAINST THE TRADITIONAL THEOLOGY

As we have already seen, Tillich's aim was to establish a harmonious relationship between the Christian faith and modern society. It is, however, important to note at once that this aim did not exclude theological criticism, but, on the contrary, implied a sharp critical judgement of modern civilization and also had, as one of its most important consequences, a distinct aversion from the traditional interpretation of the Bible and the Christian faith, which Tillich called 'supranaturalism'. Indeed, he continued in the twentieth century Schleiermacher's struggle in the nineteenth against theological 'supranaturalism'. But what is supranaturalism?

This theology presupposes a view of nature which has come into prominence in modern (natural) science and which is quite different from what the Greek philosophers understood by *physis* and the Romans by *natura*. Within the scheme of modern science that has developed in Europe since the sixteenth and seventeenth centuries, nature is seen as a network of causal relationships. Everything that occurs must be explained, insofar as it can be explained, from the natural relationships, from known or still unknown natural laws. Supranaturalism was the theological defence against this idea of reality, which amounted to, or at least seemed to amount to, an assault against fundamental theological notions such as Providence and the miracles. There is, it was said, not only a chain of natural relationships—God is also present. Generally, he uses natural causal relationships to achieve his will, but he can also, wherever and whenever he wants to, by-pass these natural causes, with the result that there are not only natural events, but also supernatural occurrences— miracles, which refer to God's Providence and to his power over nature. This supranaturalism is therefore a phenomenon which has only revealed itself in the past few centuries of European history and it is consequently confusing whenever the Bible is called a supranaturalistic book—it simply cannot be!

According to the theology of supranaturalism, God is the

one who made the world five thousand years ago or even longer, the time is not important. He did not create the world without a purpose. He had a plan for the world which is always being furthered and realized. There are moments when God intervenes in the world to overcome resistance and to accomplish his plan for the world. It is at such moments that miracles take place—as, for example, the great miracle of Christmas, when the virgin Mary gave birth to the Son of God, and the other great miracle of Easter, when the grave was found to be empty and the crucified Christ again met his own. There are also the small, but no less important miracles, in which God's Providence is made apparent in every human life. Eventually, he will have accomplished his plan for the world and that will be the end, the consummation. There is, then, in the supranaturalist conception of the world, a series of supernatural events within and in addition to the natural event.

Tillich rejected this scheme of God's relationship with men which was, and in many cases still is, for very many people, identical with the Christian faith (with the consequence that they are unable to imagine what faith would be without it!), just as Schleiermacher had done in the nineteenth century. Theology has to recognize the indissolubility of the structures of the finite world—Providence is something quite different from intervention!—and to accept the naturalist criticism of the traditional theology without falling into naturalism, which (so long as there is still a question of God) identifies him with nature, as in the case of Spinoza: 'Deus sive natura'.

All this has important consequences for theology, Christology, eschatology, our understanding of God's Providence and so on. I shall come back to these questions in the last part of this book.

THE 'PROTESTANT PRINCIPLE'

In the *Systematic Theology,* Tillich was firmly opposed not only to supranaturalism, but also to what could be called 'suprahistoricism', that is, to any refusal to recognize the historical character and the inevitable ambiguity of all historical phenomena, including the Bible, the Church, dogma, liturgy and so on. This was a consequence of what Tillich himself called the 'Protestant principle'. Various formulations of this principle can be found in Tillich's work (not only in the *Systematic Theology*). It includes, among others, the following elements:

1. the infinite distance between God and man, which cannot be bridged by men ('God is in heaven, and you are upon earth', *Eccles.* 5: 2);

2. that man is justified *sola gratia*, 'by faith alone', and not on the basis of his (good) works, in other words, that, in the relationship between God and man, only God can act and man can only accept that God has accepted him;

3. the conviction that man, even though God has accepted him and has, so to speak, given him a true basis to his life, is still man and leads his own life in alienation from reality—he has not become a saint, but remains involved in the ambiguity which is peculiar to human life, an ambiguity which he transcends, but does not abandon;

4. the conviction, closely related to the foregoing, that no human, historical and terrestrial reality can presume to have the last word and that any state or Church that does presume to have the last word must be resisted.

The Protestant principle, then, is a rejection of all heteronomy, such as that of the Middle Ages, of seventeenth-century Protestant orthodoxy and of traditional Roman Catholicism, not in the name of any autonomy, which is bound, in the long run, to result in nihilism, but in the name of theonomy.

The Protestant principle is therefore in conflict with the deification—Tillich would call it the demonization—of any terrestrial element despite its 'ambiguity'. In using the word 'Protestant', Tillich was, moreover, not implying that this 'principle' was only to be found in Protestant Christianity. He saw this principle actively at work in the prophets of the Old Testament, in their struggle against the sacral monarchy, the priest and the temple. It was prominent in the Reformation. Its action can be detected here and there in a completely secular society and it can also make itself felt in Roman Catholicism whenever Catholic Christianity 'is more open to the demand for reformation than are the churches of the Reformation'.[1] The appearance of Pope John XXIII could be interpreted as a coming to light of the 'Protestant principle' in Roman Catholicism without implying that this great pope was ever really a Protestant. In a word, then, the Protestant principle means that there is not any authority in this world which has the ultimate word—not the Church, not Luther, not Thomas, not Augustine, not even the Bible, not the state, morality, not even order. Only God alone, who speaks to men not only through the testimony of the Bible and through tradition, but also through the seeking of their own hearts and answers the question that is their own lives, even if they have not experienced it as a question—only God has the last word.

It is not pure chance that this survey of the reconnoitrers should begin with Paul Tillich. He was a man who lived on the frontier—this was how he himself described his life shortly after leaving Germany in 1933 and it is also a good way of characterizing the *Systematic Theology*.

On the one hand, Tillich felt himself to be very closely connected with theological tradition and he tried, in the *Systematic Theology*, to include all the great symbols of the Christian faith in a setting which, in its formal structure, strongly resembles the classical dogmatics of the seventeenth century. If we try to fit him into van Peursen's 'model' of the history of human thought (see page 10), we have to place him on the frontier between the second and the third stages and say that his *Systematic Theology* still has a decidedly metaphysical character (in the sense in which metaphysics is used by van Peursen, not in the sense in which the word is defined on page 28 of this book). Tillich believed that we could make do with a fundamental reconstruction of the solid building of

[1] *Op. cit.*, III, 4.

dogmatics. This makes him, seen in the light of further developments, a thinker on the frontier. Finally, Tillich's dialogue with philosophy was a dialogue with Heidegger and, what is more, with the Heidegger of *Sein und Zeit*, published in 1927, and not with the later Heidegger. As a result, the *Systematic Theology* makes an almost antiquated impression.

On the other hand, however, there are many aspects of Tillich's life and work which make him a very modern figure. In the first place, there is his opposition to all 'supranaturalism' in theology, to all fundamentalism—even in the form in which it recurs in the work of Karl Barth—and to all the miraculous events which, for many people, still form the essence of Christian faith. There is also his firm conviction that the Christian faith should not be allowed to take place in a self-enclosed, autonomous world, but must be situated in the middle of the *Universitas scientiarum*, in dialogue with the humane sciences and especially with philosophy, so that it does not become degraded to the level of a timeless activity like that of Archimedes on the beach at Syracuse. Furthermore, there is the great emphasis with which he pointed, especially during the period when he was a religious socialist at the time of the Weimar Republic, to the need for social and political commitment on the part of those who live in the new reality, in which men who live in Christ and in the community of his Spirit participate. Finally, if we also include the radical nature of Tillich's life and thought in the light of the Protestant principle, it should no longer surprise us that Thomas Altizer and William Hamilton dedicated their collection of essays, *Radical Theology and the Death of God*, published shortly after Tillich's death, to the memory of this theologian on the frontier.

Rudolf Bultmann

BIBLIOGRAPHY

RUDOLF Bultmann was born in 1884 and wrote a great deal, but the most important of his writings in the context of the new theology are those which deal with the so-called 'demythologization' (*Entmythologisierung*) of the New Testament and preaching. His essay 'Neues Testament und Mythologie', published in 1941 in the collection *Offenbarung und Heilsgeschehen*, gave rise to the violent debate for and against 'demythologization'. This essay appeared later in an American translation in *Kerygma and Myth*, published by Harper of New York in 1961. This book includes not only Bultmann's essay 'The New Testament and Mythology', but also a number of criticisms of Bultmann's views by Julius Schniewind, Ernst Lohmeyer and Helmut Thielicke among others.

The discussion is continued in the later volumes of *Kerygma und Mythos*, which have been published in German by Herbert Reich, Evangelische Verlag GmbH, Hamburg (II, 1952; III, 1954; IV, 1955; V, 1955; VI, 1, 1963). Like the first collection of essays, the second volume includes a number of criticisms of 'demythologization' by, among others, Karl Barth. It also contains an article by Bultmann himself, entitled 'Zum Problem der Entmythologisierung' (pp. 179-208), in which Bultmann throws more light on his earlier essay of 1941 and makes a number of clearer formulations.

Kerygma und Mythos III contains Karl Jaspers's dialogue

with Bultmann about demythologization. This has also been published separately by R. Piper of Munich in 1954, under the title of *Die Frage der Entmythologisierung*. Volumes IV, V and VI, 1 of *Kerygma und Mythos* are less important.

Bultmann himself gave a good summary of his views concerning the demythologization of the New Testament and preaching, in his Shaffer Lectures delivered in 1951 at Yale University. These lectures were published in 1953 by Charles Scribner's Sons of New York as *Jesus Christ and Mythology*. They were also included in Rudolf Bultmann, *Glauben und Verstehen*, Volume IV, published by J. C. B. Mohr (Paul Siebeck), Tübingen, 1965, pp. 141-89. Anyone wishing to find his way for the first time in the work of Rudolf Bultmann would be advised to begin with this little book of less than a hundred pages.

A rather more extensive publication which is not directly concerned with demythologization is the collection containing his Gifford Lectures on history and eschatology given in 1955 at Edinburgh University. These lectures were published in 1957 by the Edinburgh University Press as *History and Eschatology*.

The picture that emerges from these writings can be amplified by the other essays by Bultmann that have been published by J. C. B. Mohr (Paul Siebeck) of Tübingen under the title of *Glauben und Verstehen* (I, 1933; II, 1952; III, 1960; IV, 1965). The most important of these relating to demythologization is 'Das Problem der Hermeneutik', which can be found in Volume II of *Glauben und Verstehen* (pp. 211-35).

A good introduction to Bultmann's thought will be found in Walter Schmithal's book, *Die Theologie Rudolf Bultmanns*, published by J. C. B. Mohr of Tübingen in 1966. The book is the result of lectures given in the Studium Generale of Marburg University and was written at a fairly popular level. Bultmann himself is given every opportunity to speak in this book and Schmithals's critical commentary is kept to a minimum, with the result that the reader can gain quite a good impression of Bultmann's theology. Certainly no better introduction to Bultmann's thought exists at the moment. Also worth reading is the chapter devoted to Bultmann in H. Zahrnt's *Die Sache mit Gott. Die protestantische Theologie im 20. Jahrhundert*, R. Piper, Munich, 1966, pp. 260-325.

In order to complete this bibliography of Bultmann's works, I should also mention three other books which are monuments of biblical scholarship and milestones in the study of the New Testament, but which do not contribute very much to the specific theme of demythologization. These are *Die Geschichte der synoptischen Tradition*, a study of the origin of the so-called synoptic gospels, Matthew, Mark and Luke, published in 1921; a great commentary on the Gospel of John, published in 1941; and *Theology and the New Testament*, published by the SCM Press, London.

My intention, in attempting to demythologize the Bible, is not to make faith attractive to people of the present age by critically touching up tradition or biblical statements, but to make clear to these people what Christian faith is and thus to confront them with the choice, the decision that faith invites. My intention . . . is to make the 'stumbling-block', the σκάνδαλον of the problem of faith, clear not only to people of the present age, but quite simply to man. This means that my reason for attempting this demythologization is certainly also to get rid of those stumbling-blocks which stand in the way of people of the present age because they live with an image of the world that is conditioned by science. In undertaking this task, my principal aim is not to reassure people of the present age by telling them, 'You need no longer believe this and that'. Certainly, that is also the case, and that is why this undertaking can also free people from a burden that weighs heavily on their consciences. If this does happen, however, it will not happen because it has been demonstrated that the amount that has to be believed is less than has always been thought, but because it has been demonstrated that believing is something fundamentally different from accepting a greater or lesser number of assertions. By making the meaning of 'faith' clear, demythologization confronts people with a fundamental choice . . . It seems to me that this is the only thing and at the same time the most important thing that the theologian can do—to show what Christian faith is and with what fundamental decision it is concerned . . . His task is to reveal the question which God puts to man and which is the great stumbling-block for natural man. This is the great demand that is made of him—to renounce all certainty that he would like to achieve. The real problem is therefore the hermeneutical problem—it is a question of interpreting the Bible and preaching so that they can be understood as a word that addresses and calls man.[1]

The following quotation is taken not from Bultmann, but from a nineteenth-century theologian, David Friedrich Strauss.

My opponent himself admits that I wish to preserve the essence of the Christian faith. Must the man who, in dangerous circumstances, wishes to preserve the essence of a cause and is prepared to let the non-essential go, be regarded as an enemy of that cause? It is, of course, true that Dr Steudel and I do not agree about what the essence of faith is, but I could, with equal justice, reverse the accusation and call him, from my point of view, an enemy of faith. The servant who takes the worn-out clothes from his master's house when it is on fire and leaves the jewels to be destroyed in the flames could equally well be charged with behaving as an enemy towards his master.

The book, *Das Leben Jesu kritisch bearbeitet* (1835-6), caused a great storm because in it Strauss denied the historicity

[1] R. Bultmann, and K. Jaspers, *Die Frage der Entmythologisierung*, Munich 1954.

of the New Testament accounts and attributed them to 'unintentionally educative legend'. These accounts, then, were, in Strauss's view, myths, but these myths were the expression of the Idea, and this Idea—the unity of God and man—was the essence of the Christian faith. It was therefore not Strauss's intention to eliminate the myths from the New Testament, but to interpret them so that they became, as it were, transparent and enabled the eternal Idea that was present in them to be seen.

An avalanche of criticism descended on the book and on the head of its author, that Judas Iscariot of the nineteenth century, that enemy of faith. One of the critics was Dr Steudel, a professor at Tübingen, who took up the cudgels for the authority of Scripture and therefore(!) for the historicity of the New Testament tradition. Strauss replied to his critics in his *Streitschriften zur Vertheidigung meiner Schrift über das Leben Jesu und zur Charakteristik der gegenwärtigen Theologie* (1837). It is from the first of these polemical writings, his reply to Dr Steudel, that I have quoted the extract containing the little parable of the master and his servant. The house is on fire. The Church's teaching contradicts the 'modern' image of the world. In these 'dangerous circumstances', there are two possibilities—either to rescue the jewels from the fire and leave the worn-out clothes to be burnt, in other words, preserve what is essential, or to try to preserve everything and then be left holding the worn-out clothes in one's (empty) hands in a world that is bound to reject this faith.

Bultmann's situation is very similar to that of David Friedrich Strauss. He too lives in 'dangerous circumstances' in which the credibility of the gospel and of the Christian message is at stake and he too is confronted with the dilemma of the jewels and the worn-out clothes. In his case, the jewels are the kerygma, the proclamation of the message that addresses men and calls them to a life of faith, and the worn-out clothes are the mythological image of the world of the New Testament in which the kerygma comes to us. His fundamental theme is thus accurately stated in the two words kerygma and myth. The great difference between Strauss and Bultmann, however, is this. Strauss found the philosophy of idealism, and in particular that of Hegel, the best means to help him to distinguish the essence of faith (the 'Idea') from its mythical embellishments, whereas Bultmann found this means in Heidegger's *Sein und Zeit I* and, in his case, the essence is consequently not the Idea of the eternal unity of God and man, but the happening and liberating kerygma.

It is possible to say that Bultmann is concerned with only one thing—to show what Christian faith is and what it is not. This aim is very clearly stated by Bultmann in the passage quoted above from his discussion with Karl Jaspers about 'Die Frage der Entmythologisierung'.

It is, moreover, clear from the above passage that Bultmann does not regard the Christian faith as the acceptance of a number of statements about God, man, the world, nature and history, but as a decision which changes the whole of life and which is the response to the kerygma, the 'word that addresses and calls man', and to the question that God puts to us in the kerygma. Expressed in a simplified and schematic form, we may say that, whereas Tillich reflected about man who asks about Reality and about the answer that is given to him in the symbols of the Christian faith, Bultmann reflects about God who crosses our path with a question and about the answer that we give him or refuse to give him. Our answer, the response that we *de facto* live out in our lives, is faith.

We may also conclude from the passage quoted that faith is always and for all people a σκάνδαλον, something that is contrary to nature and goes against the ordinary pattern of life, with the result that it always and for all people means a separation and a new beginning, death and a new life. Without being what is known as *converted* in the traditional theology, a man may well be religious, but he cannot believe! Bultmann's intention in demythologizing cannot therefore be to make faith attractive and to clear the σκάνδαλον, the stumbling-block or scandal—and here he is going back to

Kierkegaard and, beyond Kierkegaard, to the New Testament (see *Matt.*: 11:6; 13:57; 26:31, 33; 1 *Cor.* 1:23, etc.) —out of the way of modern man. No, for him, either faith is a complete break with the old pattern of life or it is not faith at all in the sense in which the gospel uses the word.

There are, however, stumbling-blocks for twentieth-century man which are closely connected with the fact that, in the course of the centuries, faith has deteriorated into the acceptance by man of a number of assertions about God, man, the world and so on, and, above all, with the fact that we now live with an image of the world that is different from that of the Old and New Testaments. Our image of the world is conditioned by modern science. The ancient image of the world, on the other hand, was not scientifically conditioned, but mythological. These stumbling-blocks, Bultmann insists, have now to be cleared out of man's way, because they are 'in no way specifically Christian'—they are David Friedrich Strauss's worn-out clothes. The conversion that leads to faith is in no sense a conversion to the ancient image of the world.

The theologian's one task, Bultmann maintains, is to show what Christian faith is. Theology has no power to make people believe. That is an existential choice which has to be made by every individual

> and no one ever knows the words of God
> unless they come to him from God himself
>
> M. Nijhoff.

The theologian's task, then, is simply to remove the stumbling-blocks from the path that can lead to faith. He can only clear debris out of the way—but he must do this.

There is little to say about Bultmann's life. He was born in 1884 in the Lutheran minister's house in the little village of Wiefelstede near Oldenburg. He was a pupil at Oldenburg grammar school at the same time as Karl Jaspers, who was a few years older than he was. Afterwards, he studied theology, first at Tübingen and later at Berlin and Marburg. In 1916, he became Professor extraordinary at Breslau. In 1920, he left Breslau and went to Giessen to succeed the famous Wilhelm Bousset. In 1921, he went to Marburg as Professor of New Testament Studies and Early Christian Religious History. It was in Marburg, in 1924 and 1925, that he got to know Paul Tillich and Martin Heidegger, who was at that time working on his *Sein und Zeit*. Heidegger's philosophy was of decisive importance to Bultmann, who dedicated the first volume of his *Glauben und Verstehen* to Heidegger 'in grateful memory of the time that we spent together in Marburg'. His friendship with Heidegger came to an end in 1933, when Heidegger became a National Socialist and Rector of the University of Freiburg. At this time, Bultmann was close to Karl Barth and to the circle that had formed around the journal *Zwischen den Zeiten*, to which Bultmann contributed various articles. Later, however, the distance between Barth and Bultmann increased. Barth saw little more in Bultmann's demythologization than a continuation of the liberal theology of the nineteenth century, and that was an error. Bultmann's life passed without any further dramatic events. Although he was an opponent of the Third Reich and made no secret of the fact—for example, he spoke out clearly against the *Arierparagraph* (the German legal enactions passed in the nineteen-thirties relating to the Aryanization of the German people)—he was allowed to carry on his work at Marburg until he was honourably discharged from service in 1954.

CONFLICTING IMAGES OF THE WORLD

THE situation in which twentieth-century man hears the gospel is one in which two images of the world are in conflict with each other. On the one hand, there is the biblical image of the world, which is, as a general rule, unthinkingly perpetuated in most Christian preaching. This is the mythological view of the world. On the other hand, there is the conflicting modern image of the world, based mainly on the findings of modern science. In this situation, the question that faces us is, must the biblical image of the world also be accepted together with faith, or is it possible to believe within the framework of the modern world-image? Bultmann's answer to this is, 'To demythologize is to deny that the message of the Bible and the Church is tied to an ancient and outdated view of the world.'

But what *is* a mythological image of the world? Bultmann's own definition of the word myth will not help us very much here, because he makes use, in his definition, of too many other terms which themselves require further definition. Rather than allow ourselves to be held up by his definition, however, let us try to describe the mythological image of the world, at least in very broad outline. People live on this earth. Above them is heaven and under their feet is hell. God lives in heaven. He is almighty and he rules the world. That is to say, he intervenes in the events that take place on earth —leading his people out of Egypt and into the promised land of Canaan and so on, breaking through the order of nature and history and making himself felt in an 'open' world. Confronting God is the devil. Ranged alongside God are the legions of angels, whereas the devil has his demons and 'spirits'. The decisive event is that God has sent his Son, 'born of the Virgin Mary', who has conquered the demons and opposed the devil and who was crucified 'according to the definite plan and foreknowledge of God' (*Acts* 2:23) and his grave is empty. He descended into hell and ascended into heaven and is seated at the right hand of God. He will later return 'on the clouds of heaven' and that will be the end of history and of the great separation. In the meantime, the holy Spirit does his work on earth, in the Church and through the sacraments, and the angel of the Lord smites Herod (*Acts* 12:23).

Is this the gospel? Is this what we have to believe, although it is in conflict with the whole of our contemporary image of the world and the whole of our experience of reality? (There are no angels and no demons and miracles do not happen. God was not in Auschwitz and Hitler was not smitten by an angel of the Lord.) Anyone who claims that this is really the gospel, that the Church has to say this and that people have to believe this, is confusing the kerygma—which still sounds through all this—with a host of out-of-date mythological ideas. He is blocking the way, for people of this present age, to faith, truth and freedom.

Theology has therefore to distinguish and separate from each other firstly the kerygma and secondly the mythological image of the world. This is the task of 'demythologization'. It is not a question of eliminating the myths from the gospel, but of interpreting them in such a way that they become transparent, with the result that their real intention can be seen.

If we wonder what the 'worn-out clothes' are, Bultmann's answer to this is, heaven and hell, the *descensus ad inferos,* the ascension into heaven, Christ's second coming, faith in spirits and demons, belief in miracles, the mythological expectation of the future, the New Testament view of the holy Spirit and the sacraments, the idea of death as a punishment for sin and the idea of Christ's death as satisfaction for sin which brought death into the world, Christ's pre-existence and his birth of the virgin Mary, his resurrection from the dead as a rising again from the (empty) grave and even God himself 'in the old sense' of the God who rules the world from his heaven, has his plan for the world and so on.

This does not mean that we have to tear a number of pages out of the Bible—those parts, for example, dealing with the birth of Christ and the Christmas story, the miracles and the resurrection, and Paul's account of sin and death in Romans 5. If that were so, we should have to tear almost everything out. No, we do not encounter myths here and the kerygma there in the New Testament. There is no place in the New Testament where the kerygma is to be found separate from mythological ideas and there is no place where mythological ideas are to be found that are pure myth. Just as hydrogen and oxygen are combined with each other in H_2O, so too are kerygma and myth combined with each other in the New Testament.

DEMYTHOLOGIZATION

THIS situation makes demythologization necessary. Demythologizing the New Testament is not eliminating all the mythological ideas, accounts and elements from the New Testament—to do this would be to have nothing left at the end! No, it is interpreting these ideas, accounts and elements so that they become transparent and their real intention is thereby revealed. It is, then, simply a question of interpreting the text of the New Testament with the aim of finding out what the text really means, although it would at first sight appear to mean something quite different:

> But look, things are not what they seem
> M. Nijhoff.

Bultmann was convinced that the New Testament text intends to speak (and does speak) about man and about the transcendent 'unworldly' power, which at the same time establishes and limits human existence, about God. But because the text intends to speak (and does speak) about human existence, 'demythologization' is connected with a term that is reminiscent of Heidegger, *Existenzialinterpretation*. It is important to note that Heidegger's term *Existenzial-* refers to the structure of the state of being man, as such, and not to the specific choice, plan and decisions made by each individual person, for which we may here use the word 'existential'. It is in the former sense of *Existenzialinterpretation* that Bultmann believed that the New Testament should be interpreted, not in the latter, 'existential' sense.

The difference between *Existenzial-* and 'existential' can best be made clear by a few simple examples. A man can tell the truth or he can lie. Whether he does the one or the other is his 'existential' choice. But he can only do the one or the other because being able to speak itself belongs to the *Existenzial-* structure of the state of being man. To take another example, a man can worry about his future or he can confidently go forward to meet the future. Whether he does the one or the other is, at least partially, his own 'existential' choice. But he can only do the one or the other because knowing about the future and being ahead of oneself in the future belong to the *Existenzial-* structure of the state of being man. In *Existenzialinterpretation,* then, it is not a question of understanding 'existentially' the kerygma—that is, faith—but of discovering the understanding of, or insight into, self (*Selbstverständnis*) that is expressed in the New Testament by the use of mythological ideas and themes. Thus, whereas a man responds *in faith* to the question that God puts to him (this is an 'existential' event), the *Existenzialinterpretation* describes the structure of the existence in faith which he discovers by patiently listening to the text of the New Testament and by going beyond this and listening also to what is really intended (and indeed said!) in the New Testament. Or, when a man persists in his own pattern of life and refuses to respond to God's question (and this is also an 'existential' event), the *Existenzialinterpretation* describes the structure of the life in sin, the life outside faith. Neither of these structures are tied to the mythological ideas and elements in which the New Testament conceived them, nor are they tied to the time at which the New Testament was written. Both these structures go back to the single basic structure of human existence, an adequate description of which Bultmann found in the *Existenzial-* analysis which Heidegger provided in his *Sein und Zeit I.*

The question of demythologization as an *Existenzialinterpretation* of the New Testament is therefore, how does the New Testament speak about man and how does it speak about God? It is, after all, not possible to speak about man without also speaking about God, and it is impossible to speak about God without also speaking about man. Bultmann was thus able to say that demythologization is a hermeneutic method, that is, a method of interpretation. Hermeneutics have, from time immemorial, been a systematic reflection about the method and the rules of interpreting (written) texts.

SIN AND FAITH OR DEATH AND LIFE

BULTMANN describes the two structures of human existence in his essay on the New Testament and Mythology in *Kerygma und Mythos I*, in which he makes use of Heidegger's terminology, which he 'rediscovers' in the New Testament.

1. Outside faith, man falls back on the visible and tangible world and on everything that is available to him and that he can and wishes to have at his disposal (*das Verfügbare*). His life becomes, to use Heidegger's term, which Bultmann also found in the New Testament (see *Matt.* 6:27 f.=*Luke* 12:24 f.; *Matt.* 13:22=*Luke* 8:14; 1 *Cor.* 7:32 ff., etc.), care or anxiety (*die Sorge*), that is, a search for certainty and security and, in all this, self-preservation. His life without faith is at the same time fear which, in a lucidity that is without illusion, sees through all supposed certainty and security and causes him to become even more a victim of care and to fall back even more on what is available to him. 'In fear, everyone tries to hold on to himself and to what belongs to him, but secretly knows that everything, even his own life, escapes him.' Man is thus a prisoner, isolated and alienated from true Life, in a treadmill. He must . . . He is subject to the Law, to sin and he can do nothing else. Life is death.

2. Faith frees man from this fatal treadmill of care and fear. Free for his fellow-man and free for the future, he lives now from *das Unverfügbare*, from what is not available to him or at his disposal, the invisible, intangible reality that is more real than anything else, from God. To describe this freedom —which is nothing but simple obedience to God's call—Bultmann made an unfortunate choice of word, saying that, through faith, man became *entweltlicht*. He did not mean, however, that, in accepting faith, man bade farewell to the

world as such, but that man, in faith, bade farewell to the old world, the old treadmill life of care and fear, and at the same time came to live in the presence of God and men in terrestrial history. Bultmann called this new life the 'eschatological' existence, implying that, for him, eschatology was no longer concerned simply with the 'last things' and future events, but with the 'new creation' (2 *Cor.* 5:17) which gives men faith and Life itself.

Finally, how does man leave his old world and enter this new world? How does he leave death and enter life? The *sola gratia*, 'by grace alone', of the Reformation can be clearly discerned in Bultmann's answer to this question—a man can *only* get out of the vicious circle of sin by the liberating action of God. The essence of the New Testament kerygma is that God liberates man by entering his life and constituting the eschatological existence. That is, according to Bultmann, the fundamental difference between the New Testament and all philosophy, even Heidegger's: 'The New Testament speaks about, and the Christian faith knows of, an act of God by which faith and love, man's real Life, are first made possible.'

THE ACT OF GOD

SOMETHING must be said in conclusion about Bultmann's conception of this act of God since, until we know what he meant by it, we shall remain in mythology. Like Tillich, Bultmann does not see the act of God as a divine intervention in the order of nature and history. On the other hand, he does not think of it as analogous to human actions. God's action is not an assault made on the 'closed' relationships of our lives and of history. It is the happening and liberating kerygma itself which sets free here and now those men who allow themselves to be set free. God does not perform any miracles, but, in a world without miracles, the great miracle is that God speaks. 'In the beginning was the Word' (*John* 1:1). Thus, alongside the Protestant *sola gratia*, Bultmann places the equally Protestant *sola Scriptura*—Scripture alone, the word alone, breaks through 'the mute circle of existence'.

The kerygma speaks about the Christ who was crucified and who rose again. In the New Testament, the crucifixion of Christ, which was a historical event, and the resurrection, which, as the return of the crucified Christ from the grave in which he was laid, was a 'mythological' event, are overgrown with mythological ideas. Here too, demythologization, as an *Existenzialinterpretation,* must make the mythological ideas transparent. The crucifixion and resurrection are not 'facts of salvation' which precede faith. Belief in the cross means that a man takes up himself the cross of his parting from his old world, that he loses his life to God. And belief in the resurrection means that he himself rises to a life in freedom and in faith and love.

Unlike Tillich, Bultmann founded a school during his long period of work at the University of Marburg. Among the New Testament scholars who are prominent in Germany at the moment, there are many of Bultmann's disciples, including, for example, Ernst Käsemann and Günther Bornkamm. Although they are critical of Bultmann—they criticize, for example, his indifference to the historical Jesus—they are nonetheless only concerned with the kerygma of the crucified and resurrected Lord. They go farther, however, along the road pointed out by the great master. Bultmann's demythologization and hermeneutics have also aroused considerable interest in America, especially in the case of James M. Robinson, but also in the case of those theologians whose work has a more systematic and dogmatic character, such as Schubert M. Ogden and Paul van Buren.

Questions about the hermeneutics of the New Testament are, of course, always being raised in Bultmann's school. Two of his disciples, Gerhard Ebeling and Ernst Fuchs, have consequently devised a systematic theological plan which is generally known as the new hermeneutics. This will be discussed later in this book.

Bultmann's thought is unmistakably radical, perhaps even

more radical than that of Tillich. This is probably why *Kein anderes Evangelium* has, up to the present, directed its attacks against Bultmann especially. All the same, it is possible to say—and Bonhoeffer said it—that we must go farther than Bultmann, because Bultmann's work is still a document of a 'religious' interpretation of the gospel and because history, moving from the past towards the future via human decisions, seems in this case to fall into the *Geschichtlichkeit* (the word is untranslatable; it is briefly explained on p. 157) of the individual confronted by God, with the result that freedom in Christ, that new reality of faith, threatens to become a freedom without history and without social and political shape. The one is connected with the other. But what is a 'religious' interpretation of the gospel? If we are to understand this, we must listen to Dietrich Bonhoeffer.

Dietrich Bonhoeffer

BIBLIOGRAPHY

OF all the writings of Dietrich Bonhoeffer (1906-45), those which were edited after his death by Eberhard Bethge are the most important for the new theology. These are his unfinished *Ethics*, translated by M. Horton Smith and published by the SCM Press, London, in 1955 and *Letters and Papers from Prison*, translated by R. H. Fuller and first published by the SCM Press in 1953, a third, revised edition appearing in 1967. Bonhoeffer's most important notes on the 'religionless' interpretation of the Bible will be found in his letters dated 30 April 1944, 5 May 1944, 25 May 1944, 8 June 1944, 27 June 1944, 8 July 1944, 16 July 1944 and 18 July 1944 and in the outline of a book which appears in his letter of 3 August 1944. These eight letters and the outline form the Magna Carta of much of the new theology.

For the further study of Bonhoeffer's work, a great deal can be found in his *Gesammelte Schriften*, also edited by Eberhard Bethge. The four volumes of these collected writings have been published by Chr. Kaiser Verlag of Munich (I, 1958; II, 1959; III, 1960; IV, 1961). Nothing contained in these volumes is, however, as important as the two books mentioned above.

Because Bonhoeffer's notes on the religionless interpretation of the Bible were no more than a beginning and a first reconnaissance and because they only provide an indication of what was (still only vaguely) in his mind, the articles and books that have been written about Bonhoeffer are, to a great extent, expositions and interpretations of these 'enigmatical utterances', as Karl Barth called them. The most important of these essays have been collected and published in four volumes with the title *Die mündige Welt* by Chr. Kaiser Verlag, Munich (I, 1955; II, 1956; III, 1960; IV, 1963). One of the most outstanding contributions to this collection is Gerhard Ebeling's 'Die nicht-religiöse Interpretation biblischer Begriffe' (*Die mündige Welt II*, pp. 12-73).

One of the most important books about Bonhoeffer is that written by his friend, Eberhard Bethge (to whom Bonhoeffer wrote most of the letters collected in his *Letters and Papers from Prison*): *Dietrich Bonhoeffer. Theologe—Christ—Zeitgenosse,* published by Chr. Kaiser of Munich in 1967. Bethge has, with great care, assembled all the data about Bonhoeffer that he could lay his hands on and, with this material, has written a book that is a running commentary on Bonhoeffer's writings.

John A. Phillips's book, *The Form of Christ in the World,* published by Harper & Row of New York in 1967 with the new title, *Christ for Us in the Theology of Dietrich Bonhoeffer,* provides a brief survey of Bonhoeffer's theology from *Sanctorum Communio* (his first book) up to and including the *Letters and Papers from Prison.*

Heinrich Ott's book, *Wirklichkeit und Glaube, I: Zum theologischen Erbe Dietrich Bonhoeffers,* was published, also in 1967, by Vandenhoeck und Ruprecht of Göttingen. Ott here deals with the latest development in Bonhoeffer's thought, in other words, with the *Ethics* and the *Letters and Papers from Prison,* and attempts to go further along the road which Bonhoeffer pointed out. It is difficult to read, but it is one of the most exciting books about Bonhoeffer that has so far appeared, especially in those places where Ott tries to link together Bonhoeffer's vision of the future with that of Teilhard de Chardin.

A review of the studies about Bonhoeffer up to 1961 can be found in A. D. Müller, 'Dietrich Bonhoeffers Prinzip der weltlichen Interpretation und Verkündigung des Evangeliums', *Theologische Literaturzeitung* 86, 1961, (pp. 723 ff.) and

6

a review of the 'directions' in the interpretation of Bonhoeffer has been provided by Rudolf Schulze in his 'Hauptlinien der Bonhoeffer-Interpretation', *Evangelische Theologie* 25, 1965, (pp. 681-700).

What is bothering me incessantly is the question what Christianity really is, or indeed who Christ really is, for us today. The time . . . of inwardness and conscience—and that means the time of religion in general—is over. We are moving towards a completely religionless time; people as they are now simply cannot be religious any more . . . If therefore man becomes radically religionless—and I think that that is already more or less the case . . . —what does that mean for 'Christianity'? . . . What kind of situation emerges for us, for the Church? How can Christ become the Lord of the religionless as well? Are there religionless Christians? If religion is only a garment of Christianity . . . then what is a religionless Christianity? . . . The questions to be answered would surely be: What do a Church, a community, a sermon, a liturgy, a Christian life mean in a religionless world? How do we speak of God—without religion, i.e. without the temporally conditioned presuppositions of metaphysics, inwardness, and so on? How do we speak (or perhaps we cannot now even 'speak' as we used to) in a 'secular' way about 'God'? In what way are we 'religionless-secular' Christians, in what way are we the ἐκκλησία, those who are called forth, not regarding ourselves from a religious point of view as specially favour-ed, but rather as belonging wholly to the world? In that case Christ is no longer an object of religion, but something quite different, really the Lord of the world. But what does that mean?[1]

This fragment from a letter which Bonhoeffer wrote on 30 April 1944 in prison at Tegel, Berlin is no more than a series of questions. Some of the people who were given the

[1] C. Bonhoeffer, *Letters and Papers from Prison*, London 1967, 152-3

small volume of his letters and notes to read in 1951 must have been puzzled by it, especially if they were not acquainted with Karl Barth's *Church Dogmatics II,* Parts 1 and 2 and Barth's arguments about religion and (Christian) faith. What was Bonhoeffer's aim? What did he mean by a Christianity without religion, a 'religionless' Christianity, in a world that had moved away from metaphysics, from 'inwardness', from the conscience and so on and thus(?) also from religion? And what was he thinking of when he spoke about a religionless interpretation of the Bible in other letters?

In looking for an answer to these questions, we have very little material at our disposal—only eight or ten letters, written within a period of less than four months, a total of about forty to fifty pages of text. All that we possess, then, is a fragment, an initial reconnaissance of entirely new theological possibilities. We cannot say with certainty—we can only guess how Bonhoeffer continued to think about these new possibilities during the last few months of his life. We have only a few fragments from which the whole of his thought can be to some extent deduced, and this only in broad outline. These letters and notes form just such a fragment.

We are bound to conclude from the letters and notes themselves that Bonhoeffer himself did not know for certain, and that in his writings he was feeling his way in absolute loneliness towards a 'new' faith. Karl Barth called them 'enigmatic utterances', but, although this may well be the first word, it certainly cannot be the last word to be said about Bonhoeffer's *Letters and Papers from Prison.* It is at least possible to obtain from his book a picture of his vision. The key to the puzzle is surely to be found in what Bonhoeffer meant by religion. Once we have established this, we can also perhaps understand what a religionless world is (Bonhoeffer also speaks of a world that has 'come of age') and what a religionless interpretation of the Bible is and ultimately also what Christian faith in any case is not—and perhaps even what it is.

It is unfortunately impossible to discuss here the question of the continuity and (or) discontinuity of the *Letters and*

Papers with Bonhoeffer's earlier writings, however important this may be for our interpretation of the book. There is in any case continuity in that, throughout his whole life, he called the Church to what he called 'concrete secular responsibility' in the history of the world. The *politeia* of believers is, despite Philippians 3:20, here on earth, and the Church, 'those who are called forth' (this is Bonhoeffer's interpretation of the Greek word (ἐκκλησία), is something 'belonging wholly to the world'.

Bonhoeffer was still a young man when he was put to death by the S.S. in the spring of 1945. He was born in Breslau, in 1906, the son of the Professor of Psychiatry at the University. He studied theology, from 1924 until 1928, at Berlin. One of his teachers there was the renowned historian, Adolf von Harnack (d. 1930). In his *Letters and Papers,* he describes himself as a modern theologian, that is, as a theologian who has taken part in the revolution brought about in theology by Karl Barth, but who still carries with him the heritage of the liberal theology. After completing his studies, he worked, from 1928 until 1929, as a vicar among the German community in Barcelona. He returned to Berlin in 1929, where he was a chaplain to the students of the Technical University and at the same time a 'private' (unsalaried) lecturer at Berlin University. During this period, he did a great deal of work in the ecumenical sphere among young people and in 'Life and Work' and for the Christian peace movement. When Hitler came to power in 1933, he was involved in the struggle of the Confessing Church of Germany against the so-called 'German Christians' who submitted to the new régime. He was, however, unexpectedly appointed minister to the German community in London in the autumn of 1933, to the great annoyance of, among others, Karl Barth. He returned to Germany in 1935 and took charge of the theological seminary of the Confessing Church at Finkenwalde. When this seminary was closed by order of the German government in 1937, Bonhoeffer continued to work in the Confessing Church and also became deeply involved in the German resistance movement. After the failure of an attempt on Hitler's life in the spring of 1943, he was taken prisoner. His last journey began in the military prison at Tegel, Berlin. Eighteen months later, he was placed in closer confinement in the Gestapo prison in the Prinz-Albrecht-Strasse in Berlin. Later he was removed to the concentration camp at Buchenwald, then to Schönberg and finally, on 8 April 1945, to Flossenbürg. His last letter from Berlin is dated 17 January 1945.

Whereas Tillich was principally concerned with dogmatic theology and, in this study, with the question of the relationship between modern civilization and Christian faith, and Bultmann with the New Testament, Bonhoeffer worked all his life on problems concerned with ethics. This is borne out by *The Cost of Discipleship* (SCM Press, London 1937), a study of the theme of the *imitatio Christi* in the gospels, his unfinished *Ethics* (1955), which was edited after his death by Eberhard Bethge, and the notes in his *Letters and Papers*.

ON THE WAY TO AUTONOMY

IN the late Middle Ages, Europe abandoned the authoritative medieval pattern of life and began to move towards a new world in which men were no longer to live and believe on the authority of a Church, but were to lead their own lives as people 'come of age'. 'The autonomy of man and of the world is the aim of all thought'—this is how Bonhoeffer summarized seven centuries of European history in a single sentence.

In describing the modern world as a world come of age, Bonhoeffer was probably thinking of Kant's definition of the Enlightenment in the essay, 'Was ist Aufklärung?', published in 1784 in the *Berlinische Monatsschrift*, in which he called the Enlightenment man's farewell to the immaturity for which he had only himself and his own cowardice to blame, and man's listening and response to the call: *sapere aude*—take the risk and rely on your own intellect. The revolutions of the

nineteenth century marked the end of this venture and the
world of the twentieth century is the world come of age.
This is Bonhoeffer's first thesis and it forms the point of
departure for his further reflections.

This thesis is not refuted by the fact that most people in the
twentieth century in Western Europe and America do not
lead their own lives and belong far more to the 'radar' inner-
directed type described by David Riesmann in *The Lonely
Crowd*. Nor is it proved wrong by the fact that the twentieth
century in Europe has been a period of totalitarian régimes
—something which certainly did not escape Bonhoeffer's
attention. It was precisely because European man had been
looking, during the period of the Enlightenment and even
long before this, for a way out of Kant's immaturity for
which man had only himself to blame (*selbstverschuldete
Unmündigkeit*) and because at the same time he had done too
little towards democratizing European society—he naturally
wanted to cling to the ancient order and did not want to burn
his boats behind him—that the totalitarian leader and the
radar-type, who mutually presuppose each other, were able
to emerge. Bonhoeffer's coming of age (*Mündigkeit*) is at the
same time a fact, in the sense that man recognizes no
authority that he does not experience as 'authentic'. It is the
most succinct formula for the autonomy which Bonhoeffer
had in mind and which is not in conflict with Tillich's
theonomy. It is also a task which man has to undertake with
realism and perseverance.

Here we must pause for a moment to consider a concept
that plays an important part in the letters, the concept of
'intellectual honesty'. Although the authority of Christianity
is fast disappearing all around us and coming of age is, in
this sense, a fact, intellectual honesty has still to be found. It
will begin with the straightforward acceptance of the fact
that we have to live in this situation and that we cannot, in
this situation, fall back on a God who will simply clarify
everything when we have come to the end of our understanding. That God is no longer there. He has forsaken us. What

Bonhoeffer especially valued in Bultmann, shortly after the publication of his 'New Testament and Mythology', is that he gave a hearing to the demands of intellectual honesty which are made to us in our present situation. Bonhoeffer did not find this intellectual honesty in the Confessing Church.

In the context of the old Europe, bidding farewell to immaturity meant forsaking religion, the Churches and also 'God'. In this sense, Bonhoeffer's conclusion is inevitable: 'We are moving towards a completely religionless time'. We cannot go back to the old Europe—we can only go forward on the difficult road towards the future and freedom. We must not even wish to go back and must resist the longing expressed in the words of the German song which Bonhoeffer quotes in this context: 'If only I knew the way back, the long way back to the land of childhood'.[1] The old security lies behind us, for ever.

RELIGION AND RELIGIOUS CHRISTIANITY

Now that we have established this, we must try to discover what Bonhoeffer meant by religion. The difficulty here is that he never defined the word religion and confined himself to describing it with words such as metaphysics, inwardness and so on, which he also did not define. In addition to the few data to be found in his *Letters and Papers*, there are several others, as, for example, the note in his *Ethics*, in which he wrote about the 'pietism' and the purely religious preaching which separates the gospel from man's secular existence in history. It is from these few data that a model of religion in the sense in which Bonhoeffer understood it must be constructed. This is, broadly speaking, as follows.

Man lives in the world with his questions, his fears, his confusions and his uncertainties and he knows of his guilt and of approaching death. In this situation, he is powerless and he appeals to God, who has all power and 'who does everything according to his dear will' as Valerius has said in

[1] *Op. cit.*, 196.

his *Gedenckklank*. God can and does listen to him, by forgiving him, by giving him bread to eat and by providing him with the prospect of life after death. Insignificant and powerless man has found God's almighty help. There is a way out of life on earth with death as the ultimate horizon and out of man's discouraging experiences with himself and with his fellow-men. There is a heaven, a future, a *Hinterwelt* (Nietzsche) and inwardness. There is also opium, to use Karl Marx's word, although I have not found this extreme formula in Bonhoeffer.

All this and more can be said. Religion comes within man's horizon at the point where he is at the frontier, in what Karl Jaspers has called frontier situations—death, grief, guilt and so on. It is not to be found in the middle of life, where man is strong and knows how to manage. Religion is somewhere on the fringe of life, where it exists as a separate 'religious quarter' alongside ordinary life, where those who 'labour and are heavily laden' can find a place. God finds a last shelter in this 'religious quarter' after he has been cast out of the world and man too finds in this quarter the rest that his restless heart is seeking.

Apologetics also belonged, in Bonhoeffer's opinion, to religion. He regarded apologetics as an attempt to convince men that they cannot live without God and without religion and that they are essentially always, even if they do not know it themselves, on the frontier, in a desperate situation in which the choice lies between Jesus and despair. Karl Heim, Bonhoeffer maintained, tried by pietistic methods to convince man that he was faced with the alternative, 'Jesus or despair'. Existentialism and psychology were also introduced in order to convince man that his situation was really so desperate that he could not find an explanation himself, to convince him therefore that the pilots were ready to bring him into the haven of faith. Bonhoeffer was of the opinion that the attack on the world's coming of age by Christian apologetics was in the first place meaningless, in the second place unimportant and in the third place unchristian.

That is more or less how Bonhoeffer understood religion, a view which Gerhard Ebeling has excellently described as 'the complementing of reality by God'. Bonhoeffer himself paraphrased it in a little poem which incidentally shows that he was not a poet:

Men go to God when they are sore bestead,
Pray to him for succour, for his peace, for bread,
For mercy for them sick, sinning, or dead;
All men do so, Christian and unbelieving.[1]

Behind this criticism of religion, we are aware of the presence of Karl Barth who, in his *Epistle to the Romans* and his *Church Dogmatics I*, Part 2, Chapter 17, argued that religion had been 'cancelled out' by Revelation. There are, however, differences between Bonhoeffer and Barth. Whereas for Barth religion was a systematic and dogmatic construction, for Bonhoeffer it was the name for a number of phenomena in German (and not only German) Protestantism of past centuries which were distasteful to him. Neither Barth nor Bonhoeffer, however, claimed to have said anything essential in connection with Islam or Buddhism, for example, because both of them were opposed only to religious 'Christianity'. A second difference is even more important. Barth believed that religion was an essentially human phenomenon, which meant that there could be no question of a world without religion—work will always go on in the blacksmith's shop where man forges his idols. Bonhoeffer, on the other hand, regarded religion as a historical phenomenon which would eventually disappear and for him the twentieth century was the period of the disappearance of religion. Consequently, then, 'we are moving towards a completely religionless time'.

Bonhoeffer was therefore clearly aware of standing at a turning-point in history. However great the problems of the industrial revolution or of world population 'explosion' might be, neither of these phenomena constituted for him the

[1]*Op. cit.*, 200.

fundamental event of the twentieth century. For Bonhoeffer, this was the end of religion and of the religious interpretation of life and history. This in turn raises further questions. Is the end of religion also the end of Christianity? The answer is obvious and cannot be avoided—it does mean the end of Christianity, at least so long as Christianity is a religion. Is it?

Bonhoeffer's first thesis was that the religious period of human history was coming to an end. His second thesis, however, closely related to the first, was that the Bible has, up to the present, always been interpreted in the Churches in a 'religious' sense, that is, as the answer to man's questions, fears and confusions and as the way out of history towards the true Life that is found elsewhere. In other words, the Christian faith has so far always come to us in the garment of religion. The end of religion is therefore also the end of traditional, religious Christianity. Or ought we to say that it is the end of Christianity pure and simple?

Before we go into this question, however, we must ask another one—is the end of religion also the end, the death of God? Once again, the answer is obvious and cannot be avoided—the end of religion is indeed the death of 'God'. A world without religion is a world without 'God'. Was Nietzsche right then when he proclaimed the gospel of the death of God in *Die fröhliche Wissenschaft* and *Also sprach Zarathustra*? Yes, he was right, but Bonhoeffer insists, 'The world that has come of age is more godless, and perhaps for that very reason nearer to God, than the world before its coming of age'[1] (in his letter of 18 July 1944). For Bonhoeffer, just as for Heidegger (although Bonhoeffer probably had not read Heidegger), the death of 'God' could be the beginning of a new theophany. And so the end of religious Christianity could be the beginning of an authentic Christian *faith*.

THE RELIGIONLESS INTERPRETATION OF THE BIBLE

'Jesus calls men, not to a new religion, but to life,' Bonhoeffer

[1] *Op. cit.*, 200.

wrote in the same letter of 18 July 1944. That life—we might
also say faith—is not a new religion and the Bible is not a
religious book. The religious interpretation of the Bible was
an obscuring of what the Bible really meant. But, we may
object, surely the Bible, just like religion, is concerned with
forgiveness and with redemption from death and surely Jesus
calls men 'who labour and are heavy laden' (*Matt.* 11:28)
so that rest is given to them? Is that a new religion or should
it be called life itself? There does not seem to be very much
difference.

The letter of 27 June 1944 takes us a stage further. After
referring to the difference between the Old Testament and
the 'other oriental religions', in which connection he was
probably thinking especially of Egypt, Bonhoeffer went on
to say: 'To the objection that a crucial importance is given
in the Old Testament to redemption (from Egypt, and later
from Babylon—cf. Deutero-Isaiah) it may be answered that
the redemptions referred to here are *historical*, i.e. on *this* side
of death, whereas everywhere else the myths about redemption are concerned to overcome the barrier of death. Israel
is delivered out of Egypt so that it may live before God as
God's people on earth. The redemption myths try unhistori-
cally to find an eternity after death.'[1] The Old Testament,
then, is concerned with this earth and with history. One
might also say, as Bonhoeffer did himself, that it is concerned
with 'righteousness and the kingdom of God'.[2] No escape
from history is offered, no opium is provided, but a people is
made capable of living in authentic historical responsibility.

That is the Old Testament. Is it different in the New
Testament? What about the unity of the Old and New Testaments? Surely various things are said in the New Testament
about resurrection and a life beyond death? Bonhoeffer
denied that the traditional interpretation of the theme of
resurrection was relevant. 'The difference between the
Christian hope of resurrection and the mythological hope is

[1] *Op. cit.,* 185.
[2] *Op. cit.,* 156.

that the former sends a man back to his life on earth in a wholly new way which is even more sharply defined than it is in the Old Testament.'[1] Man, the earth and history all belong intimately to each other. 'This world must not be prematurely written off; in this the Old and New Testaments are at one.' Here and nowhere else is Life itself.

In recent years, there has been a great deal of speculation and much has been written, by Rudolf Bultmann and others, about the need for and the impossibility of what has been called an exegesis 'without presuppositions'. The need is clear—the Bible must be allowed to speak for itself and to say what it has to say. The impossibility is also very clear— the Bible is always read and understood in the light of certain assumptions that are generally not carefully thought out and penetrated. Bonhoeffer was the first to realize that the Churches have for centuries read their Bible in the light of one single, enormous assumption which they have never really noticed and have consequently never critically examined. This assumption is that the Bible answers—and that God, in the Bible, answers—man's religious questions, and that the Bible is consequently a religious book. Now that this assumption has ultimately been thought out and seen through, a religionless interpretation of the Bible has at last become possible, and not only possible but also necessary, so that we may at last see what Life itself is.

It should now be clear why Bonhoeffer was able to say that Bultmann had not carried his demythologization far enough —he left the religious interpretation of the Bible quite intact. Bonhoeffer, however, went even farther and read the Bible in the light of a new and religionless interpretation. In this light, all the words of the Bible acquire a different meaning, even such elementary words as God, faith, and so on. His basic thesis was to listen patiently to all the words of the Bible and to re-interpret them from a new point of view. This new horizon was that the Bible speaks along the path of the people of God in the history of this world, on their way

[1] *Op. cit.,* 186.

towards the kingdom and righteousness. Anyone, however, who is on the way towards the kingdom of God and righteousness and who thus lives in faith (a faith that has nothing to do with religion) is bound to encounter suffering on his way. Bonhoeffer, of course, experienced great suffering in his own life, but the suffering of those who follow Christ is not only present in the extreme situation of the Third Reich, but is also always present whenever people are called from their old world and respond to this call. It was therefore not his own circumstances, the particular situation in which he found himself while he was writing his *Letters and Papers,* that happened to lead to suffering playing such an important part in Bonhoeffer's thought. Suffering may not be essential to religion, but it is certainly essential to faith. Jesus was first and foremost the suffering servant of Yahweh (*Is.* 53), who was 'despised and rejected' for the sake of the kingdom and righteousness, who was nailed to the cross and who is crucified again in the least of his brothers, so that we are bound to agree with Pascal when he said, in his *Mystère de Jésus,* 'Jesus will be in agony until the end of the world . . .' In Bonhoeffer's 'theology of the cross', God himself is also not the Adonai of Isaiah 6, raised up high above men on his throne and surrounded by the singing of seraphim, those beings of smoke and fire, but the God who suffers in this world and 'lets himself be pushed out of the world on to the cross'.[1] For Bonhoeffer, God is only God in this way.

It is therefore hardly surprising that faith, 'following' Jesus (we recognize here the author of *The Cost of Discipleship*), should be characterized by suffering. Faith, for Bonhoeffer, is letting oneself be carried away by Christ along the path that he followed and in the messianic suffering of God. All our 'religious' questions and cares only stand in our way and prevent us from doing justice, from being righteous. Both doing justice and sharing in God's suffering are inseparable in faith and together they constitute the life to which we are called by Christ. In the passage that I have quoted above,

[1] *Op. cit.,* 196.

Pascal adds '. . . we must not be asleep during that time' and Bonhoeffer also wrote about 'watching with Christ in Gethsemane'[1] in one of his letters (21 July 1944).

We can state exactly how far Bonhoeffer got—his *Letters and Papers* were no more than a beginning, a tentative orientation. They tell us something about his new, religionless interpretation—a number of rather vague hints—but hardly anything about the new meaning that the words of the Bible should have within the framework of this interpretation. In the chapters on Christology and ecclesiology, later in this book, a little more will be said about this.

But what those 'who are called forth' are to do is at least as important as what the Church is to say. Perhaps everything simply cannot be said and perhaps there is much that can only be done. Jesus calls those who have been called forth, not to a new religion, nor to a new doctrine about God, man and the world, but to Life itself. And what that means can be expressed in a single sentence, once again taken from the poem, 'Christians and Pagans', quoted previously:

> Christians stand by God in his hour of grieving and they stand there strong, courageous, ready to resist, knowing what is at stake and suffering with God for the sake of righteousness.[2]

Will there be a Church and will there be Christians in a religionless world? There will, only if the Churches abandon their religious interpretation of the gospel, because, at the turning-point of history, the time of religious Christianity is past. There can only be a future for a Church which commits itself to history in this world for the sake of *šālôm* and righteousness and Christ's sovereignty. But what does this mean?

In his lonely meditations, Bonhoeffer was sustained by a great confidence in the future. 'It is not for us to prophesy the day (though the day will come) when men will once more

[1] *Op. cit.*, 202.
[2] *Op. cit.*, 200.

be called so to utter the word of God that the world will be changed and renewed by it. It will be a new language, perhaps quite non-religious, but liberating and redeeming— as was Jesus's language; . . . it will be the language of a new righteousness and truth, proclaiming God's peace with men and the coming of his kingdom.'[1] Until that day comes, we must wait and do what we have to do. The situation is reminiscent of that of Isaiah and his disciples at the time of the sealing of the Torah (*Is.* 8: 16–17).

Very soon after their publication, Bonhoeffer's *Letters and Papers from Prison* evoked an enormous response not only in Germany itself, but also—despite the great power that the 'religious establishment' still possesses in those countries—in England and America. Even in the Far East, Bonhoeffer's *Letters and Papers* have been translated and have become the subject of study. His name will occur again and again in the chapters that follow, sometimes in connection with those of Tillich and Bultmann, sometimes in other connections.

---

[1] *Op. cit.*, 172.

The New Hermeneutics

BIBLIOGRAPHY

MOST of the work of Ernst Fuchs and Gerhard Ebeling has, up to the present, consisted of articles published in various journals, especially in the *Zeitschrift für Theologie und Kirche*. Some of these articles have been collected and published in book form. J. C. B. Mohr of Tübingen, for example, published a collection of Ebeling's essays, dedicated to Hans Rückert and Ernst Fuchs in 1960, a second edition appearing in 1962. This collection is called *Wort und Glaube* and includes the great study of the religionless interpretation of the Bible which is mentioned in the bibliography on Bonhoeffer. J. C. B. Mohr has also published three volumes of Ernst Fuchs's collected articles: *Zum hermeneutischen Problem in der Theologie. Die existenziale Interpretation* (1959), *Zur Frage nach dem historischen Jesus* (1960) and *Glaube und Erfahrung. Zum christologischen Problem im Neuen Testament* (1965).

It will be clear simply from the titles of these volumes that there is a connection between the new hermeneutics and the work of Rudolf Bultmann. In 1962, Gerhard Ebeling dedicated a little book, *Theologie und Verkündigung. Ein Gespräch mit Rudolf Bultmann* (J. C. B. Mohr, Tübingen), to the dialogue with Bultmann. Another little book by Ebeling, however, *Das Wesen des christlichen Glaubens* (J. C. B. Mohr, Tübingen, 1959), is more suitable as an introduction to Ebeling's thought. It includes a number of lectures given by Ebeling within the framework of the Studium Generale at Zürich between 1958 and 1959 and a broadcast talk given over South German Radio in 1959. A cheap edition of this book was published in 1964 by the Siebenstern Taschenbuch Verlag. Finally, I should mention a collection of sermons on the Our Father, entitled *Vom Gebet* and published by J. C. B. Mohr in 1963 and the book *Gott und Wort*, published by J. C. B. Mohr in 1966. *Gott und Wort* contains the three lectures which Ebeling gave in Berkeley, California and in which he discussed, among other things, the theology of the death of God.

In addition to the three volumes of Ernst Fuchs's collected essays mentioned above, I must also mention his *Hermeneutik*, published in Bad Cannstatt in 1954 (third edition in 1963). Like everything else that Ernst Fuchs has written, this book is difficult to read and anyone who wishes to familiarize himself with the new hermeneutics is recommended to begin with Gerhard Ebeling, *Das Wesen des christlichen Glaubens*, being, as I have already said, the most suitable introduction.

The New Hermeneutic, a book published in 1965 by Harper and Row of New York as Part 2 of the series *New Frontiers in Theology*, contains a discussion about the new hermeneutics and provides an instructive survey of the developments in hermeneutics since the appearance of Karl Barth's *Epistle to the Romans*. This survey is written by James M. Robinson. Other contributions are by Gerhard Ebeling, Ernst Fuchs and various American theologians, including John Cobb Jr. The book also contains Fuchs's reply to the Americans.

An excellent outline of Ebeling's theology will be found in *Tendenzen der Theologie im 20. Jahrhundert. Eine Geschichte in Porträts*, published by Kreuz Verlag, Stuttgart, and Walter Verlag, Olten, 1966, pp. 589–96. The portrait of Ebeling was written by the editor of the book, Hans Jürgen Schultz.

Now for a few biographical details. Ernst Fuchs was born in 1903 and studied theology and philosophy under, among others, Rudolf Bultmann in Marburg. In 1932, he worked as a 'private' (unsalaried) lecturer at Bonn and, in 1933, he became a preacher in Württemberg. In 1949 he was a

7

lecturer and in 1951 he was Professor in New Testament Studies at Tübingen. In 1955 he became Professor in New Testament Studies at the Kirchliche Hochschule of Berlin and in 1960, Professor in New Testament Studies and Hermeneutics at Marburg, thus succeeding to the chair that Rudolf Bultmann had occupied for so long.

Gerhard Ebeling, who was born in 1912, also studied theology and philosophy under Bultmann in Marburg. He was a student, too, in the seminary for preachers of the Confessing Church in Finkenwalde, where he met Bonhoeffer. In 1939 he was a preacher in an emergency parish of the Confessing Church in Berlin. During the war, between 1939 and 1945, he was a medical orderly in the German army. In 1946 he became Professor of Church History at Tübingen. In 1954 he became Professor of Systematic Theology, also at Tübingen and in 1956, Professor of Systematic Theology, the History of Dogma, and Symbolism at Zürich. In 1965 he returned to Tübingen. In 1963 and 1966, he lectured in the United States.

Ernst Fuchs and Gerhard Ebeling got to know each other at Tübingen between 1949 and 1955. This was of decisive importance for both of them, for it was in those years in Tübingen that the new hermeneutics originated.

The proclamation of the Christian message is such an exceptionally difficult task in our own times because the language of that proclamation is today experienced as a foreign language. The words are known and so are the sentences formed with these words. Many people have become so familiar with them that they no longer give very much thought to them and are in any case no longer provoked by them to surprised reflection. It is possible that this meets with approval here and there and that it is seen as a criterion of orthodoxy. But what it has to do with the reality around us remains obscure. To take the fact that we know what the Christian faith is in itself as our point of departure and then to add to this that this faith must be

brought into relationship with the reality of our own times
—this is impossible. What is at stake in the Christian faith
is simply to understand it when our reality is involved in
it and not when something is said afterwards about that
reality. In the Christian faith, what is at stake is simply
this reality of our own times and nothing else. We, however, have formed the habit of allowing the proclamation
of the Christian faith to speak about a different reality and
then afterwards (at least so long as everything goes all
right!) of asking how all this is related to our reality.

Christianity has become acquainted with life in two
spheres—in the sphere of the Church and in the sphere of
the world. And it has become acquainted with the fact that
two languages exist side by side—the Christian language
with its venerable patina of twenty centuries and the
language of the reality in which we are living. It does occasionally happen that the spark jumps across and that
there is real understanding. But we have no comprehensive
text-book for translation in our bilingual situation. It is
hardly necessary to say that this problem is far too great
for us to be able to solve it by borrowing words from
modern jargon and using them for the language of the
Christian faith. It is not a question of understanding a
number of words, but of understanding the Word itself. It
is not a question of new media of language, but of a new
coming to language.[1]

The situation within which Ernst Fuchs and Gerhard
Ebeling are working is the same as the situation within which
Tillich, Bultmann and Bonhoeffer worked, but their new
hermeneutics are a different answer to this situation. It is
clear from the passage quoted above that Ebeling, like
Tillich, Bultmann and Bonhoeffer, is opposed to the idea that
it is possible for us, independently of our situation—independently of the reality—first to determine what Christian

[1] Gerhard Ebeling, *Das Wesen des christlichen Glaubens*, Siebenstern Taschenbuch Verlag, 1964, 13, 14.

faith is in order to ask afterwards what that Christian faith has to say about this situation. Anyone setting about the task in this way is bound to begin by making faith into a timeless, self-enclosed world and the Church into a ghetto. We know then what Christian faith is, even though what it has to do with the present reality or whether it has anything to do with this reality at all will remain for the time being obscure. This was the view of the Christian faith to which Tillich objected with his method of correlation, Bultmann objected with his demythologization and Bonhoeffer objected with his religionless interpretation of the Bible. 'The situation cannot be excluded from theological work'—Fuchs and Ebeling are entirely in agreement with this, even though they do not follow the author of the *Systematic Theology* on his way towards a correlation of philosophy and theology, of question and answer and even though the name of Tillich does not occur in their writings.

The passage quoted above is therefore more reminiscent of Bonhoeffer than of Tillich. Bonhoeffer believed that the Confessing Church had remained faithful to the fundamental Christian concepts and was therefore capable of resisting contamination of the Christian faith by Germanic mythology. But he criticized the Church at the same time for not having interpreted these concepts, with the result that what she had to say was, for most people, remote from life itself and remained 'undisclosed'. Ebeling had heard this criticism and agreed with it. In the above fragment and in the whole of Ebeling's work, there is much more that is reminiscent of Bonhoeffer—it is evident that, after their meeting in Finkenwalde, Ebeling observed Bonhoeffer closely.

All the same, Ebeling and Fuchs are more at home among Bultmann's ideas than among Bonhoeffer's, and the new hermeneutics may be roughly defined as a variation of the *Existenzialinterpretation* of Bultmann. Ebeling dedicated an entire book to the dialogue with Bultmann, and Fuchs gave his first volume of articles the sub-title: Die Existenzialinterpretation.

What we have seen so far of the new hermeneutics can be summarized in a single sentence by Ebeling himself: 'Our task is not to insist on a definite interpretation that has been given to us, but to insist on the never-ending interpretation of the gospel.' True Christian faith is not firmly anchored to the formulas of the past—it must be looked for and found again and again in what Fuchs has called the 'event of language' and Ebeling the 'event of the Word', in which faith once more 'comes to language' and light shines over our present reality.

OLD AND NEW HERMENEUTICS

I MUST now map out the relationship between Bultmann and the new hermeneutics in a little more detail and, to do this, I can begin with the fragment quoted above from Gerhard Ebeling's book, *Das Wesen des christlichen Glaubens*.

1. It is clear from this fragment that Ebeling shares with Bultmann the theme of *Glauben und Verstehen*, believing and understanding. Faith is an understanding of myself and of the world, in one word, of the reality, in the light of the Word of proclamation. There can therefore be no question of finding faith in a sacrifice of the intellect, in accepting on authority what can only be accepted in this way and then regarded as valid, as truth, without being understood and without any connection with the reality of life, nor does faith lie in relinquishing the very desire to understand what is thus believed. On the contrary, faith is precisely an understanding of self and of the world (in other words, of reality) in a new way and no longer in the light of the past, but in the light of the future, an understanding in which, in addition to the word faith, words such as love, freedom, future and so on are heard—the same words that we met in the case of Bultmann.

2. It is also clear from this fragment that faith has nothing to do with a number of timeless truths which can probably be added to a 'Christian' view of the world, so that the task of dogmatics would be to systematize these truths about God,

man and the world, nature and history, and so on. Words like 'event of language' and 'event of the Word', as used by Fuchs and Ebeling, point in a different direction. They indicate that faith is a response to, or comes about as the result of, an 'event', in other words, as the result of the Word of God, which is an act of God. They indicate too that faith, as a response to this event, has an existential character. Faith has nothing to do with a set of truths, but everything to do with the truth that is God himself.

3. Finally, it is also clear from this fragment that both Fuchs and Ebeling are, as Bultmann himself was, concerned with the preaching of the gospel to people of the modern age, people who have once and for all time been estranged from the 'mythology' of the New Testament and who can only come to faith and to themselves through the kerygma of the New Testament. Ebeling defines theology succinctly and well as 'concern for proclamation' and that is the only 'concern' that theology has. Theology has no more to do than simply to serve the proclamation of the gospel in the world of our own times as well as possible. Its task is interpretation, even *Existenzialinterpretation,* so as to enable a language with its 'venerable patina of twenty centuries' to become an 'event of language' for the modern age.

4. What Ebeling does not say explicitly in this fragment (not because he wished to remain silent about it, but because there was no occasion to mention it here) but what is certainly implied in all that has been said so far is this: Christian faith is not a faith in miraculous events like the return of the crucified Jesus from the grave in which he was laid. It is rather, in imitation of Jesus, the witness who is at the same time the basis of faith, a sharing in Jesus's freedom and obedience and courage in God's proximity and, in all this, the 'travelling of being on the way' towards the kingdom. The fact that Ebeling has more to say about faith in this context and Fuchs more about love is a very small difference in comparison with everything that they have in common.

Ebeling and Fuchs go so far with Bultmann—up to this

point, the new hermeneutics is no more than a variation of Bultmann's *Existenzialinterpretation* of the Bible. But, in theological circles, when the new hermeneutics is discussed, this name is used to distinguish the work of Ebeling and Fuchs from that of Bultmann. There are many differences, which would have to be noted in a complete survey, but here I can only point out the following.

1. Fuchs and Ebeling use the word hermeneutics in a different sense from the one in which it has hitherto been used. Hermeneutics is traditionally the theory of interpretation, the *ars interpretandi*, the 'art of understanding written statements about life' (W. Dilthey). As the theory of interpretation, hermeneutics formulates the rules that must be observed in order to understand a text—the epic of Gilgamesh, for example, or a sonnet of Shakespeare—and in order to trace the writer's intention via his words. In the 'old' hermeneutics, the relationship between the interpreter and his text is such that the interpreter tries to understand the text, or rather, via the text, the writer. In the case of Ebeling's and Fuchs's new hermeneutics, however, the situation is different. The text is not interpreted—it interprets, and it does not interpret itself, but *me* when, as an 'event of language' (Fuchs) or as an 'event of the Word' (Ebeling), it furnishes me with a new understanding of myself, of my world and possibly also of God. In the new hermeneutics, the relationship between the text and the interpreter is, so to speak, reversed. In this new situation, hermeneutics is at the service of the 'movement of language' which leads from the text—in this case, the text of the Bible—to a new 'coming to language' of the Word in proclamation as a renewing 'event of language' which changes me and my world. If theology is entirely a 'concern for proclamation', as Ebeling insists, then theology is also entirely hermeneutics.

2. On the one hand, this is the consequence of the conviction that the word of the Bible is not simply a means which men used to express their ideas, but the Word of God and this was what led Ebeling, going back to the Reformation

and especially to Luther, to his view of the Bible and of
preaching as the 'event of the Word'. On the other hand, it is
also a consequence of a theological formulation of ideas about
language taken from the later Heidegger (such writings as
Unterwegs zur Sprache) and it was along this way that Fuchs
met Ebeling. Thus the new hermeneutics originated in
Tübingen with themes derived from Luther and Heidegger.
It is therefore possible to account for the difference between
Bultmann and the new hermeneutics at least partly by the
fact that Bultmann took the concepts for his *Existenzialinterpretation* of the gospel from the younger Heidegger (of
Sein und Zeit), while Ebeling and especially Fuchs drew their
inspiration from the later Heidegger. In *Unterwegs zur
Sprache,* there is a dialogue about language in which
Heidegger himself observes that hermeneutics is not in the
first place concerned with the interpretation of texts, but,
even before this, with the 'bringing of a message and information' and, if we ask who the messenger is who brings this
message, there is only one possible answer—it is language
itself. 'The language speaks'—that is the principal theme of
an even earlier essay on language which is also to be found
in Heidegger's *Unterwegs zur Sprache*. We do not use language
in order to express our ideas—language itself presents man
himself in his essence. With this brief reference to Heidegger,
we must now return to the new hermeneutics. 'The language
speaks' and defines man in a new way. Faith lives from the
'event of language' which extends from the Bible to the
preaching of the gospel in our own times, which is a hearing
and a 'corresponding' in a new language.

3. A third difference between Bultmann and the protagon-
ists of the new hermeneutics is directly connected with this.
For Bultmann, as for Karl Barth, the historical Jesus was
outside theology. In his opinion, the Christian faith was concerned not with Jesus—that unknown quantity behind the
gospels, surrounded by legend and theology—but with the
kerygma about Jesus that is contained in the New Testament.
Fuchs's second volume of collected articles, however, bears

the title *Zur Frage nach dem historischen Jesus* (*The quest for the historical Jesus*) and we may deduce from this that Fuchs, unlike Bultmann, is interested in the new research into the historical Jesus that originated in Bultmann's school. And, in the case of Ebeling, Jesus is not simply the witness, but also the basis, the ground of faith. This is understandable. It is Jesus himself and not the kerygma about Jesus that is the decisive 'event of language' with which the history of faith—of the Christian faith—begins.

Up to this point, then, there is a certain similarity between the new hermeneutics and the work of such New Testament scholars as Ernst Käsemann and Günther Bornkamm. The quest for the historical Jesus is not, however, in the case of Fuchs and Ebeling, concerned with the facts of Jesus's life, nor with such questions as whether Jesus regarded himself as the Messiah, nor with the continuity between the historical Jesus and the Christ of the kerygma. We must try to express what was expressed in him and why he and no other is the 'event of language' that is so decisive to faith. The new hermeneutics is concerned with the fact that Jesus emerges in his words and acts from the text of the New Testament as the 'event of language' that creates life and establishes freedom. In other words, Fuchs's and Ebeling's hermeneutics are not inspired by a strictly historical interest, but by a 'concern for proclamation' in which the ground of faith (Ebeling) is sought in the 'memory' of love (Fuchs) and expressed in a new way of speaking.

FAITH—IN THE WORLD

THIS survey of the theology of Fuchs and Ebeling is, of course, like those of all the others dealt with in this book, very sketchy. But one other aspect of the new hermeneutics must still be pointed out. Fuchs and Ebeling are in agreement with Bonhoeffer's notes on the 'this-worldliness' of the Christian faith. The sphere or 'place' of faith is not a meta-physical reality beyond or behind this world, nor is it the

Church as an independent institution alongside this world. It is this world itself. 'World' in this context means the situation of twentieth-century man, who is alienated from metaphysics and mythology and who is no longer reached by the traditional expression of faith.

The passage quoted from Ebeling's *Das Wesen des christlichen Glaubens* at the beginning of this outline expresses this in clear language—'in the Christian faith, what is at stake is simply this reality of our own times and nothing else'. There is no question of there being a thinking in two spheres, Church and world (a theme from Bonhoeffer's *Ethics*). Using a variation on an idea of Fichte's, Ebeling has called the world the material of faith. Statements of this kind can also be found in the writings of Ernst Fuchs.

If, however, we look a little more closely at Fuchs's and Ebeling's texts, then the world seems to be man in his concrete situation as an individual before God (Kierkegaard), as existence. This individual before God does have a neighbour—and loving God cannot really be anything else but loving this neighbour—but the political and social structures which, as 'structures of destruction', encircle this neighbour lie outside his scope, with the result that here too love does not seem to gain any political and social outline. In other words, the questions asked by the new hermeneutics, firmly placed in the tradition of unpolitical Lutheranism, are to such an extent concentrated on the proclamation of the gospel in the situation of the individual before God that, despite its entering the world as the sphere of faith, the socio-political reality of faith is given no place in the world. In this, Fuchs and Ebeling are very close to the great master from whom they had to depart on their way towards new hermeneutics.

England

JOHN A. T. ROBINSON

Bibliography

IN 1953, the SCM Press of London brought out, in their series SCM Paperbacks, a little book by John A. T. Robinson called *Honest to God*, an outline of a new theology that was not, in every respect, entirely fortunate. The book caught on, became a best-seller and was translated into many languages.

A selection from the writings discussing *Honest to God* in England was published in the same year by the SCM Press, London. The book, edited by David L. Edwards and entitled *The Honest to God Debate, Some Reactions to the Book: Honest to God,* includes, among other things, a number of letters which Robinson received as a result of *Honest to God* and a number of reviews, including one by Rudolf Bultmann, a translation of his review in *Die Zeit* of 10 May 1963. In *The Honest to God Debate,* Robinson himself also comments on *Honest to God* in an article entitled 'The Debate Continues' (pp. 232-75) and anyone reading *Honest to God* should read this commentary as well.

A symposium, *Diskussion zu Bischof Robinsons Gott ist anders,* was published by Chr. Kaiser Verlag, Munich, in 1964, and includes, in addition to other contributions from England, the Netherlands and Germany, an article by Rudolf Bultmann entitled 'Der Gottesgedanke und der moderne Mensch'.

John A. T. Robinson has also written *Christian Morals Today* and *The New Reformation?*, both published as paperbacks by the SCM Press of London, the second in 1965. The second of these two little books, which is, in my opinion, more important than *Honest to God*, includes, among other things, a lecture by Robinson on whether it is possible for a person living *entirely* in the modern age not to be an atheist: 'Can a Truly Contemporary Person *not* be an Atheist?'

Two new books by Robinson were published, almost at the same time, in 1967. The first, *Exploration into God*, published by the SCM Press, London, in the series SCM Paperbacks, is a further elaboration of Robinson's notes on the doctrine of God contained in *Honest to God*. While still persisting in his rejection of theism, Robinson goes on in this book to argue that the relationship between God and man can only be conceived in terms of Martin Buber's I-thou relationship. The second book, *But that I can't Believe!*, which was published by Collins of London, deals with a number of misconceptions of the Christian faith.

Robinson's earlier writings, all of which deal with New Testament subjects, are of little value in connection with the new theology.

Honest to God has been criticized severely, intelligently, but, in the long run, not very convincingly by the Anglican theologian E. L. Mascall in *The Secularization of Christianity, An Analysis and a Critique*, Darton, Longman and Todd, London 1965 (especially pp. 106-89).

At the same time, I believe we are being called, over the years ahead, to far more than a restating of traditional orthodoxy in modern terms. Indeed, if our defence of the faith is limited to this, we shall find in all likelihood that we have lost out to all but a tiny religious remnant . . . The most fundamental categories of our theology—of God, of the supernatural, and of religion itself—must go into the melting. Indeed, though we shall not of course be able to do it, I can at least understand what those mean who urge that we should do well to give up using the word 'God' for a generation, so impregnated has it become with a way of thinking we may have to discard if the Gospel is to signify anything.

For I am convinced that there is a growing gulf between the traditional orthodox supernaturalism in which our faith is framed and the categories which the 'lay' world (for want of a better term) finds meaningful today. And by that I do not mean there is an increasing gap between Christianity and pagan society. That may well be so, but this is not the divide of which I am speaking . . . Indeed, many who are Christians find themselves on the same side as those who are not. And among one's intelligent non-Christian friends one discovers many who are far nearer to the Kingdom of heaven than they themselves can credit. For while they imagine they have rejected the Gospel, they have in fact largely been put off by a particular way of thinking about the world which quite legitimately they find incredible.[1]

Honest to God, a book written by a man who was unknown outside England, appeared in the spring of 1963. Its publication was an event in the world of books. This was not only because of the publicity given to it by the B.B.C. and *The Observer,* but also because of the book itself. The author was a bishop of the Church of England—a Church that clings to tradition more than any other Church in the world. These were the words of a 'guardian and defender of the faith' (this probably explains why the author refers to 'our defence of the faith' in the extract quoted above from the Preface to the book). What he was proposing was nothing less than a revolution in theology and a reformation of the Church. *Honest to God* was, of course, not the first symptom in England of opposition to the 'established' religion. Various articles had already appeared in the journal *Prism,* and in the collection *Soundings,* edited by Alec R. Vidler, which appeared in 1962, while R. Gregor Smith had written a book, *The New Man,* published in 1956, which had, alas, attracted all too little attention. But Robinson went much farther and saw more clearly what was wrong.

[1] J. A. T. Robinson, *Honest to God,* London 1963, 7–8.

Honest to God arose as a result of Robinson's experiences in connection with his work in the diocese of Southwark in South London. The situation there was not different from that in other dioceses of the Church of England and not very different either from the situation on the continent. Some people still feel at home in the Church, in the traditional formulas used for the Christian faith and in the traditional Christian way of life. But there are also people who no longer feel at home and who no longer give any thought to the matter. And there are also people who are somewhere in between these two extremes. By tradition, they belong to the Church, but they are no longer able to feel at ease in the faith of their childhood, without being able to understand why and what is wrong. And then there are others who are moving towards the Church, but are put off by many things that they cannot believe and yet are apparently expected to believe. Robinson was thinking especially of these people who are in between when he wrote *Honest to God* and he was able to write the book because he recognized himself in them—his own questions, his own doubts and his own estrangement from the old Christianity. He places his conclusion at the very beginning of the book: 'the most fundamental categories of our theology . . . must go into the melting'. He does not mean, then, that words like 'God' must disappear, but that we must re-interpret these words.

The preface to *Honest to God* tells us exactly what the theme of the book is and also what the theme of Robinson's later writings is. In the course of centuries, the proclamation of the gospel and theology have become framed in a way of thinking and in a view of the world that contemporary people—people in a secularized world—can no longer experience and accept. The image of the world that has been taken for granted for centuries is now alien and remote. What is at stake, then, is not the truth of the gospel itself, but the traditional interpretation of this truth within the framework of an old and abandoned image of the world, which Robinson, together with Tillich, call supranaturalist. I have mentioned Tillich and, indeed, Robinson's theme is, in this connection, very similar to Tillich's. There is also at least an analogy with Bultmann's demythologization, which not only applies to the New Testament, but also to the traditional preaching of the Church, and there is also an analogy with Bonhoeffer's objection to the religious interpretation of the Bible. When the matter has been carefully thought out and taken to its ultimate conclusions, there are considerable contrasts between these three theologies, but they are all united in their opposition to the contamination of the truth of the gospel with an obsolete image of the world.

These three twentieth-century theologians were therefore Robinson's guides in the revolution (which was begun with great reluctance!) in which he has taken part and which has estranged him from an atavistic theology, but not from the gospel itself. This older theology is, to use Bultmann's words, the unauthentic stumbling-block which stands in the way of faith and which must be cleared away by the new theology. What can a new terminology do, however hale and hearty or 'existential' it may be, so long as the old terminology persists?

Finally, it is clear from the passage quoted that Robinson is convinced that the future of the Christian faith and of the Church is at stake. If the older theology continues to prevail, the Church will eventually only appeal to a 'tiny religious remnant' and it will certainly not be easy to recognize in this 'remnant' the Remnant of Israel which formed the *avant-garde* of the future in the Old Testament.

It is not difficult to slate *Honest to God*, as E. L. Mascall has done. While he was at Cambridge, Robinson specialized mainly in New Testament studies and he has written books, very good books, on the Church in the New Testament and on the liturgy and eschatology. But no one can do everything, and he has given less attention to the history of theology and to dogmatics. It is pathetically obvious here and there in *Honest to God* that dogmatic thinking and the dogmatic method are not in his line. He is also not very familiar with philosophy—with existentialism, logical positivism and linguistic analysis. It is therefore clear that Robinson was not so well equipped as Tillich, Bultmann and Bonhoeffer when he set to work on *Honest to God*. But, honest in this as well, he is the first to admit it. On the other hand, however, with very clear intuition he has seen exactly where the great problems are situated for twentieth-century Christians. These questions are indeed concerned with God and his relationship with the world—the miracles, providence and the many, many questions of theodicy. They are concerned with Christ and 'who Christ really is, for us today' (Bonhoeffer). They are concerned with the Church, the liturgy and the 'religious establishment'. Finally, they are concerned with life in the world (this world!) as Christians. These are the subjects discussed in *Honest to God* and it is easy to see that Robinson, as a writer, is much closer to the man in the street than Tillich and certainly than Bultmann, the typical scholar.

THE PRACTICE OF FAITH

THERE is, however, a difference. It would be wrong to say that Tillich, Bultmann, and Bonhoeffer were directed simply and solely by a systematic interest in their work. During Tillich's German period, the whole of philosophy and theology was connected with the cause of religious socialism. Bonhoeffer's religionless interpretation of the Bible was concretely directed towards the life and suffering with God of the community in a world without religion, and even Bultmann was concerned, in his *Existenzialinterpretation* of the New Testament, with providing a greater opportunity for man's response to God's question and with faith, love and freedom. All theology is ultimately *theologia practica,* just as all faith is ultimately faith in practice, and a theology that does not fulfil this criterion has become sidetracked as theology. But Robinson is even more concerned, and certainly more directly concerned, than these theologians with practice. What is Christian action? That is his constant question and that is why the essence of *Honest to God* is not to be found in

Robinson's theological and Christological arguments or in his rejection of a God who is 'out there', but in his notes on the 'new morality'. *Honest to God* is a book that should be read from the end to the beginning. As one comes closer to the beginning, the book becomes less and less convincing.

Robinson's new morality is, in one respect, not so very new. What we have to do is simply to love. As Augustine said, 'Ama Deum et quod vis fac'—love God and then what you will, do. That is really all there is to it, and it is hardly revolutionary. But Robinson writes about the revolution in ethics and he is right. With these words, which at first sight seem so obvious, all heteronomy in ethics is shown out of the door. What I have to do, my Christian duty, cannot be looked up in a manual of moral theology with all its casuistic distinctions and it cannot be found in the Church's command- ments and in traditional 'Christian' custom. I do not live under a net of commandments that has been thrown over me, a net with a wide mesh so that I can easily slip through with a clear conscience. I have to decide myself, in freedom and autonomy and 'before the face of God', to love, which in *this* particular situation means . . . And then I have to say it myself and be answerable for what I say, without being able to appeal to moral theology and certainly without being able to take shelter behind it.

This is also not a revolution, but a consistent continuation of the Reformers' protest against Roman Catholic casuistry. Robinson, however, goes farther. In Christian action in the world, we should not refer to the ten commandments which Yahweh, according to tradition, inscribed with his own hand in the stones on Mount Sinai, or to the commandments given to us by Christ, for example, in the Sermon on the Mount, or even to the eternal and holy values that have been deduced from these. It is, for example, not possible to say that divorce is always and in all circumstances a 'sin' because Christ said 'What God has joined together, let no man put asunder' (*Matt.* 19:6). Even that is a form of heteronomy and of absence of responsibility. What I do is, in that case, not my

8

own decision—but a decision has been made for me and on me, and all that I have to do is to submit to it.

Robinson's new morality recognizes only one prescription —love. Or rather, even love is not prescribed—it is the ground of our being and it is not foreign to us. Loving is coming home! Ethics, then, are an 'ethic of the situation'. In Robinson's own words, 'Love alone . . . can allow itself to be directed completely by the situation. It alone can afford to be utterly open to the situation, or rather to the person in the situation, uniquely and for his own sake . . . It is able to embrace an ethic of radical responsiveness, meeting every situation on its own merits, with no prescriptive laws.' That, and nothing else, is the 'terrible freedom of love'.

This love, which Robinson encountered in Christ—so that the first thing that has to be said in any Christology is that Christ was, in the terrible freedom of love, 'the man for others'—is dynamite under the 'establishment'. The Church is there, not to support and maintain the existing order, but to call men to their terrible freedom.

GOD IN HEIGHT, IN DEPTH
AND IN ONE'S FELLOW-MAN

EVERYTHING that Robinson says in addition to this is no more than a series of conditions of this revolution in ethics added later. This applies to his Christological and theological notes and to everything that he says, following in the footsteps of Paul Tillich, about God as the ground of our being and as the ground of all meaning that is to be found in life. This, however, is what attracted most attention in *Honest to God,* this transition to a 'new' image of God. Rather scornful things have been said about this God in depth who should replace the God in height, up there in heaven. With little consideration for Robinson's situation, some critics have even seen a regression in his idea of a God in depth to a pre-Christian image of the world and—how in the world is it possible? —to Thor throwing his hammer through space, a god who can thus only with the greatest difficulty be thought of as a god in depth. Others, who have given Robinson a less sound thrashing, have legitimately commented that the idea of God as the ground of all being etc. has not so very many advantages over the classical image of the God in heaven.

Robinson himself did not, however, attach very much importance to these images of ground, depth and so on and realized that these replacements of the older image of the God 'out there' 'who does everything according to his dear will' were in themselves faulty. This fact emerges quite clearly from his later book, *The New Reformation?*, in which he goes much farther along the road which ends with the Christian a-theism of Paul van Buren. In *The New Reformation?*, theology is entirely taken up with Christology and God is absorbed in 'the man for others' who goes ahead of his own on the way to Emmaus. And the question is asked whether a person who lives entirely in the modern age can *not* be an atheist. The air is clearer, then, and the situation is more lucid than in *Honest to God*. What remains in *The New Reformation?* is Robinson's aversion to 'theism' and to the God of the religious tradition, and what disappears is the mystique of ground and depth, which did not really work in *Honest to God*, not even, one may suspect, for Robinson himself. It is not at all clear how Robinson's latest book, *Exploration into God*, fits into this development. It would seem as though, in this new book, he goes back, beyond *The New Reformation?* to *Honest to God* again and that the reason for this must be found in his desire to avoid the atheistic consequences which could possibly be drawn from *The New Reformation?*. This would also help to explain why he emphatically dissociates himself in this new book from William Hamilton, despite the cordial foreword that he wrote in 1966 for the second edition of Hamilton's *The New Essence of Christianity*. Nonetheless, here too, after a great deal has been said about the need for a pantheistic way of thinking about the relationship between God and the world and about the eternal Thou from whom we cannot escape, the last word is silence.

Who or what is God, then? We cannot say. We must remain silent. We have no image or likeness. God, however, does not remain silent. 'Like the disciples on the road to Emmaus, we find ourselves faced with the bewildering double adjustment of learning at one and the same time to live in a world without God and in a world with God. It is a new situation, a post-resurrection world in which the old *is* dead. There is no question of introducing that God again by the back door or of returning to the *status quo ante*. Yet, despite the irreversibility of that change, there is the constraint of the other reality with which to come to terms.'[1] The situation is that of Psalm 139.

But where does this other Reality, where does God impose himself on us? In answer to this question, Robinson refers to Bonhoeffer—the transcendent is in our fellow-man who crosses our path—and he refers to Martin Buber. And he could have referred to Gerrit Achterberg's sonnet, which begins with the line:

Man is for a time a place of God

or to Emmanuel Levinas, who said that the transcendent comes up to us in the stranger who resists the totalitarian rounding off of our world with his *extériorité* which has no place in it. He also refers to the gospel, where Christ is God's 'stadholder' and the least of his brothers is Christ's master. To serve God in the world (or rather, to live in a world with God) is, in all the situations in which life places us, really to encounter the Other, the Stranger, and to allow him to speak.

There are, of course, many questions. There is, for example, the question as to whether Robinson's new morality has room for notions like those of justice and the question as to whether God is still the entirely different one that he has been throughout the centuries. Has the barrier between God and man not been removed in this gospel that has been reduced to situation

[1] J. A. T. Robinson, *The New Reformation,* London 1965, 118.

ethics? The answer can be found in Gerrit Achterberg's poem. God, the Stranger of whom we have no image or likeness, does transcend man infinitely, but nonetheless

Man is for a time a place of God.

THEOLOGY AND LINGUISTIC ANALYSIS

Bibliography

A GOOD survey of the new 'philosophy of religion' is been written by Frederick Ferré: *Language, Logic and God,* Eyre and Spottiswoode, London 1962. This book is simple, conveniently arranged and very well documented. At the same time, it provides a historical review and a justification of theology as a meaningful discourse.

Wittgenstein's *Philosophical Investigations* (1953) is, of course, the Magna Carta of 'linguistic analysis'. The first studies on the meaning and the consequences of linguistic analysis for theology appeared shortly after its publication. Only the most important are mentioned below. In 1955, the SCM Press of London published a collection of essays edited by Antony Flew and Alasdair MacIntyre, entitled *New Essays in Philosophical Theology,* which included a fascinating discussion about 'Theology and Falsification'. Two further books appeared in 1957. These were *Faith and Logic,* a collection of essays edited by Basil Mitchell and published by Allen and Unwin of London, a reply given by a number of Oxford philosophers and theologians (all of them Christians) to the challenge of the new philosophy, and Ian T. Ramsey's *Religious Language. An Empirical Placing of Theological Phrases* (SCM Press, London). A year later, Ninian Smart's book, *Reasons and Faiths* (Routledge and Kegan Paul, London, 1958) appeared.

The new journal, *Religious Studies,* published by the Cambridge University Press, also contains a great deal of recent material on the encounter between theology and linguistic analysis. The first issue of *Religious Studies* appeared in the autumn of 1965 and included, among other things, a very clear article by Ian T. Ramsey on 'Contemporary Philosophy and the Christian Faith'.

The new 'philosophy of religion' is older than the publications of John A. T. Robinson and even older than the first signs of renewal in English theology. The most obvious consequence of the whole character of this philosophy is that it has so far aroused less of a response than the theological books and articles that I have mentioned. There is, however, every reason to expect that this philosophy will, in the near future, lead to changes in the theme of theological thinking, not only in America and England, but also on the continent. One of the first symptoms of this is Paul van Buren's book, *The Secular Meaning of the Gospel*, which will be discussed in the next chapter.

The situation is as follows. In the philosophy of the 'Viennese circle', and in logical empiricism, all ethical and metaphysical and *a fortiori* all theological statements or propositions are meaningless because their truth or falsity cannot be empirically established or because, in the idiom of this philosophy, they cannot be verified or falsified. Meaningful statements are only those of the sciences and of the basic rules of logic, which enable us to speak meaningfully. 'The rest is silence.' Beyond the frontiers of what can be said is, at the most, a metaphysics of silence. (This is, for example, the case in Wittgenstein's *Tractatus logico-philosophicus*.) The consequences of this philosophy for theology have been formulated in the following way by A. J. Ayer: 'The theist . . . may believe that his experiences provide authentic knowledge, but we can be sure that he is deluding himself unless he can express his "knowledge" in propositions which can be empirically verified. It follows that those philosophers who fill their books with assertions that they know intuitively this or that religious "truth" are only accumulating material for the psychiatrist.'

In his later writings, and especially in his *Philosophical Investigations,* Wittgenstein assigned a different task to philosophy, namely that of analysing all the 'language games' which occur in such great variety among men. We speak not one language, but many languages, and not in the sense that we speak German, French and English and perhaps Spanish and Portuguese as well, but in the sense that various situations and different contexts of conversation all have their own distinctive language game. The language of physics is, for example, different from that of jurisdiction or that of a child's song. Language thus has great logical variety. It is not the philosopher's task to say that one language is meaningful and all others are not, but it is his task to investigate the logical structure and the meaning of all these language games. One of these languages is, of course, the language of religion or theology (as a rule, no distinction is made between them). The question now is, what is the structure and what is the meaning of religious propositions? What is the framework in which they are situated and what do they 'say' within that framework?

AGAINST THEISM

ONE of the most striking consequences of this new philosophy is the rejection of the traditional Christian idea of God, the rejection of 'theism'. Ferré states quite simply in *Language, Logic and God* that this new philosophical movement cannot be associated with the older theism and T. R. Miles comes to the same conclusion in his article 'On Excluding the Supernatural' (*Religious Studies* I, 1965-6). Faced with choosing between traditional Christianity and a 'reformed' faith that excludes supranaturalism, he feels impelled to accept the second—our choice, he says, is either to accept some reformism or else to give up Christian faith altogether.

Antony Flew's 'parable' in *New Essays in Philosophical Theology,* a variation of a parable formerly devised by John Wisdom, which has become almost classical and has been quoted by Paul van Buren among others, goes even further: 'Once upon a time two explorers came upon a clearing in the jungle. In the clearing were growing many flowers and many weeds. One explorer says, "Some gardener must tend this plot." The other disagrees, "There is no gardener." So they pitch their tents and set a watch. No gardener is ever seen. "But perhaps he is an invisible gardener." So they set up a barbed-wire fence. They electrify it. They patrol with bloodhounds . . . But no shrieks ever suggest that some intruder has received a shock. No movements of the wire ever betray an invisible climber. The bloodhounds never give cry. Yet still the Believer is not convinced. "But there is a gardener, invisible, intangible, insensible to electric shocks, a gardener who has no scent and makes no sound, a gardener who comes secretly to look after the garden which he loves." At last the Sceptic despairs, "But what remains of your original assertion? Just how does what you call an invisible, intangible, eternally elusive gardener differ from an imaginary gardener or even from no gardener at all?" '[1]

This parable shows what has happened in recent centuries. Step by step, God the gardener has become so worn out that nothing is left of him. Flew's conclusion is that we can now no longer speak about God or that we can only do so by means of a kind of 'doublethink', as practised by the characters in George Orwell's *Nineteen Eighty-Four*. ('Doublethink' is the ability to hold two contradictory convictions at the same time and to accept them both. The person in question knows with his intellect that he is doing violence to reality, but at the same time he reassures himself with 'doublethink' that he has not violated reality.)

The conclusion that Antony Flew, Alasdair MacIntyre and others have come to, then, is that God the gardener has gone for good and that it is no longer possible for men to believe, in the twentieth century. Whether we like it or not, we are atheists and we have to be atheists. We cannot go back

[1]A. Flew and A. MacIntyre, *New Essays in Philosophical Theology*, London 1955, 96.

to the time before the great silence. For this reason, Alasdair MacIntyre, in an article in *Encounter*, which has also been published in *The Honest to God Debate*, criticizes Robinson for continuing to speak about 'God' and thus filling up the void of atheism, although 'God' has a completely different meaning for Robinson (but what precisely?) than the word has for traditional Christianity. For Alasdair MacIntyre, *Honest to God* is just one of the symptoms of a whole series of theologies which perpetuate a theistic terminology but which are basically atheistic. He cites Tillich, Bultmann, Bonhoeffer, Robinson and others.

Flew and MacIntyre are not Christians. They could only be Christians by means of 'doublethink' and that is only possible so long as people do not see through it. The question now is whether Christian faith is at all possible without God the gardener. What is the theologians' task in this situation? Have they to demonstrate the meaning of 'theistic' statements—which are, for MacIntyre, more or less synonymous with statements about God—as it were apologetically? Or is it possible for them to reply to the challenge of Flew's parable by a theology without God? This is, of course, at first sight absurd, yet there is a certain logic in the whole development of philosophy and theology which points in this direction, so that the experiment of a theology without God can be undertaken. But, for this experiment, we have to leave England and go over to America.

America

BIBLIOGRAPHY

IT is clear from the most recent developments in American theology that European theology is read and assimilated in America. Barth's kerygmatic theology, Bultmann's studies in connection with demythologization and above all Bonhoeffer's letters and notes of 1944 have had a deep effect. At the same time, there has also been a return to the thematic theology of the nineteenth century (this has already been noted in the case of Tillich) and Schleiermacher's name is frequently mentioned.

The most important book is Paul van Buren's *The Secular Meaning of the Gospel*, which was first published by the SCM Press of London in 1963 and in a cheap edition by the same Press in 1965. It is at present being translated into Dutch. It is not an easy book, especially for anyone who is not familiar with the principles of linguistic analysis. Dr A. J. Nijk has written an excellent summary of it in *Wending XIX*, 1964-5, (pp. 251-64), and E. L. Mascall has criticized it from the traditionally theological point of view in *The Secularization of Christianity*, London 1965.

Shortly after the publication of *The Secular Meaning of Gospel*, Gibson Winter's book, *The New Creation as Metropolis*, was published by the Macmillan Company of New York, 1963. In this book, Winter outlines the Church's task in urban society in a way which deviates radically from the traditional ecclesiology. The Macmillan Company of New York brought out a cheap edition of Winter's book in 1966. A Dutch translation, which is to be published by Paul Brand, is being prepared.

Harvey E. Cox's excellently written book, *The Secular City. Secularization and Urbanization in Theological Perspective*, appeared in 1965. This was published by the SCM Press, and a cheap edition of the same book was published in 1966 by the Macmillan Company of New York. Part of the discussion provoked by *The Secular City* can be found in *The Secular City Debate*, a book compiled by Daniel Callahan and published in 1966 by Macmillan of New York and Collier-Macmillan of London. A number of criticisms of *The Secular City* and Cox's replies to these criticisms have been brought together in this book. In a separate chapter, Cox also gives an account of his attitude towards Bonhoeffer and the religionless interpretation of the Bible.

At about the same time as *The Secular City* came out, the Judson Press of Valley Forge published another book by Cox—*God's Revolution and Man's Responsibility*. This includes a number of lectures given in 1963 and thus represents an earlier stage in Cox's thinking than *The Secular City*.

Carl Michalson's work has attracted less attention so far in Europe than the writings of Paul van Buren, Gibson Winter and Harvey E. Cox. His book, *The Rationality of Faith*, SCM Press, London 1964, must, however, be mentioned. In this book, the sub-title of which is *An Historical Critique of Theological Reason*, Michalson is mainly concerned with the method of theology, but he does also discuss what being a Christian is in the modern world.

A good impression of the most important trends in American theology can be gained from the collection *America and the Future of Theology*, edited by William A. Beardslee and published by the Westminster Press of Philadelphia in 1967.

A bibliography of books and articles connected with the 'death of God' theology will be found at the beginning of the next chapter.

In the above-mentioned review, Michalson characterizes

contemporary American theology thus: 'We are living between the times—between the time of a theology which has no more meaning for us and the time of a theology which has not yet acquired a clear form. The theology which is being written in this time between the times . . . is bound to be fragmentary and even chaotic'. We are looking, Michalson says, for the word or the words which will shed light on our road towards the time beyond this time 'between the times'. In a word, then, the situation in America is no different from that in Europe.

Michalson distinguishes four main tendencies in American theology:

1. The 'dynamic' theology which, on the one hand, is based on the philosophy of the American A. N. Whitehead and, on the other, accepts motives from Bultmann's work and elaborates them. Michalson mentions in this context Schubert M. Ogden, who makes no secret of his affinity with Bultmann in the title of his book *Christ without Myth*, and John Cobb. In this book, I can do no more than simply mention this dynamic theology.

2. The 'hermeneutic' theology, the leading exponents of which are in Europe—Michalson is no doubt thinking here of Ernst Fuchs and Gerhard Ebeling—and which is represented in America by James M. Robinson. This theology is also, on the one hand, based on the work of Bultmann and carries this further and is, on the other hand, inspired by the work of the later Heidegger, that is, not by *Sein und Zeit I*, but by such works as *Unterwegs zur Sprache*. This hermeneutic theology will similarly not be discussed in this book.

3. The secularizing theology, of which Michalson distinguishes two forms—the work of Paul van Buren and that of Harvey E. Cox.

4. The theology of the 'death of God', of which the chief exponents are William Hamilton and Thomas Altizer. This theology will be discussed in the next chapter together with the work of Dorothee Sölle.

PAUL VAN BUREN

WHERE, as one reviewer has asked of Professor Ramsey, is the transcendent God of classical Christianity? (And it is a question that we too can expect.) Have we not reduced theology to ethics? Our answer takes the form of another question: in a secular age, what would that 'more' be? It is our inability to find any empirical linguistic anchorage for that 'more' that has led to our interpretation. If this is a reduction in the content of theology, it is the sort of reduction which has been made by modern culture in many fields. Astrology has been 'reduced' to astronomy, for example; we have excluded from the study of the stars a cosmological or metaphysical theory about their effect on human life. Alchemy was 'reduced' to chemistry by the rigorous application of an empirical method. During the Renaissance, the metaphysical ideas and purposes of medieval painting were excluded, leaving 'only' the work of art. In almost every field of human learning, the metaphysical and cosmological aspect has disappeared and the subject matter has been 'limited' to the human, the historical, the empirical. Theology cannot escape this tendency if it is to be a serious mode of contemporary thought, and such a 'reduction' of content need no more be regretted in theology than in astronomy, chemistry or painting.[1]

Paul van Buren's book, *The Secular Meaning of the Gospel*, appeared after the publication of John A. T. Robinson's *Honest to God* and before the publication of his *The New Reformation?*. Van Buren expressed his agreement, with certain reservations, with *Honest to God* at the end of his book and Robinson also referred gratefully, in *The New Reformation?*, to van Buren's work, in which 'cartloads of metaphysics' were removed and the light of Easter morning shone through all the more clearly.

In the passage from *The Secular Meaning of the Gospel* quoted

[1] P. van Buren, *The Secular Meaning of the Gospel*, London 1963, 197-8.

above, van Buren admits that his interpretation of the biblical tradition is, in comparison with the rest of theology that
has so far been written, a 'reduction'. All metaphysics, all
cosmology and all that transcends the world of our experience
is excluded by van Buren, who maintains firmly that the
Bible speaks and that theology must also speak about the
human, the historical and the empirical, about man's life in
this world and in history. He does not scruple to be absolutely
agnostic in his attitude towards everything ('God' and so on)
that transcends the empirical reality.

The mutual respect that Robinson and van Buren have
for each other is connected with the fact that they both live
and think in the same situation, that is, in a secular society.
In this context, it should be noted that van Buren loosely
defines the word 'secular' as an abandonment of the idealism
of the nineteenth century and as 'a deep interest in questions
of human life this side of the "beyond" and a corresponding
lack of interest in what were once felt to be great metaphysical
questions.'[1]

Christian faith is not concerned with anything religious—
and van Buren uses the word 'religious' in the sense in which
Bonhoeffer used it—but with a human attitude in time. It is
possible to say, and indeed van Buren says so himself, that
faith is concerned with ethics. Here, he refers, among
others, to Martin Buber and his analysis of the two fundamentally different attitudes in which men can live—the
attitude of I-thou and that of I-it: 'We are urging that Buber's
distinction matters more than distinctions between eternity
and time, infinity and finite, and many other distinctions
that mattered to Christians in another age.'[2]

Van Buren's thought as an encounter with the biblical
tradition is framed within the triangle formed by Karl Barth,
Rudolf Bultmann and linguistic analysis. He agrees with Karl
Barth, under whom he studied for a time, that Christology
is the corner-stone of all theology. He shares Bultmann's

[1] *Op. cit.*, Preface, xiv.
[2] *Op. cit.*, 195.

conviction that theology must describe the Christian faith as an authentic and meaningful possibility for twentieth-century man. Finally, it is the task of linguistic analysis to ensure that man remains here on earth and in history. We are also constantly aware of the presence of Bonhoeffer and his search for a religionless interpretation of the Bible in the background of van Buren's argument, and it is certainly not by chance that the book opens with a quotation from *Letters and Papers from Prison*.

JESUS AND FREEDOM

FAITH must always be orientated towards the story of Jesus of Nazareth that has been given to us in the New Testament. In other words, theology must begin with Christology. On the one hand, van Buren aims, in his Christology, to remain faithful to what the early Church did not say but nonetheless intended to say in the Christological dogma that was defined after much controversy in 451 at the Council of Chalcedon. This dogma describes Jesus the Christ as the one who is one in two 'natures', the divine and the human (with the result that it is in him, who was crucified and rose again from the dead, that God himself and no other speaks to us). On the other hand, however, he discounts the historical enquiry into the life of Jesus of Nazareth that was recommenced in the school of Bultmann—I am thinking here especially of the studies by Ernst Fuchs and Gerhard Ebeling and of Günther Bornkamm's little book, *Jesus of Nazareth*. Van Buren wishes to remain firmly within the sphere of the human, the historical and the empirical!

For van Buren, the most essential aspect of Jesus of Nazareth was his freedom. This freedom was not undermined by care for the future (anxiety about bread to eat and so on) or by fear and self-preservation. It was a freedom which neither the sacred tradition of Scripture nor the objections of the scribes could cause to be lost. In this freedom, Jesus was able to live entirely for 'God' and entirely for men without being confused by possible consequences, isolation and the way to the cross. It was a freedom which completely unsettled the ancient world. It was a freedom which attracted and at the same time repelled men with its strange authority, because it confronted them with the abyss, the 'terrible freedom of love'. It was finally a freedom which was catching and which liberated others, Jesus's disciples, and gave them new life.

That was the day of the resurrection, the day on which the spark passed from the crucified Christ to his disciples and they knew that 'this was it' and that the whole of life could be nothing else but studies of this freedom. This response to the freedom of the crucified Christ, that was expressed, for example, in the words 'Jesus is the Kyrios (Lord)', was faith. And this faith has nothing to do with metaphysical considerations—about the infinite and the finite and so on—and everything to do with life on earth, which has once and for all time been defined by the Lord and his freedom.

Thus, Christology is for van Buren the point of departure for his interpretation of Christian faith and not for theo-logy. It is in this that he makes an important distinction, at the end of his book, between himself and Robinson, who opens his book with a dubious theology and only then goes on to speak about Christ, the 'Man for others'.

SILENCE ABOUT GOD

But what about God? It is here that *The Secular Meaning of the Gospel* is revolutionary. Van Buren insists that we must be silent about God (and silence is not the same as denial!). We can only reply to the question about God by pointing to Jesus. 'He who has seen me has seen the Father' (John 14:9) was what Jesus said to Philip in reply to his question about the Father, and Robinson had already prophesied that this text would be as fundamental for the 'new' reformation as Romans 1:17 was for Luther.

It was quite clear to Tillich, Bultmann, Bonhoeffer and Robinson that the traditionally Christian, theistic image of

God was out of date and that we have to live now without a
God who intervenes in our lives and ensures that everything
will be all right. But these writers still continue to speak about
God, about the ground of being (Tillich) and even about an
act of God (Bultmann). We must cease doing this. 'Bultmann
thinks that "modern man" can still do something with the
word "God" . . . Ogden agrees with this.'[1] Van Buren does
not, however, agree: 'The empiricist in us finds the heart of
the difficulty not in what is said about God, but in the very
talking about God at all. We do not know "what" God is, and
we cannot understand how the word "God" is being used.'[2]
This statement and other similar statements are, on the one
hand, the result of van Buren's empirical attitude and, on the
other, the consequence of his taking Barth's 'Christological
concentration' to its extreme conclusion.

Whatever the case may be, what we have here for the first
time in history is a theology without God, though we should
note at once that a theology without God is different from a
theology of the death of God and that the journal *Time* has
given rise to confusion in ranging Paul van Buren alongside
William Hamilton and Thomas Altizer. 'To-day, we cannot
even understand the Nietzschian cry that "God is dead!" for
if it were so, how could we know? No, the problem now is
that the word "God" is dead.'[3] Anyone who goes further and
talks about the death of God is making a metaphysical
statement, and that is the same as a meaningless statement.

Is this silence about God a necessary consequence of linguistic analysis? That is certainly van Buren's opinion. Is he
right? Does linguistic analysis really make speaking about
God, even in the religious or theological language game,
impossible? There is every reason to deny it. Dr L. A.
Hoedemaker has appended to his book on the theology of H.
Richard Niebuhr, *Faith in Total Life,* the assertion that Paul

van Buren has wrongly connected a linguistic analytical approach to the kerygma with the axiom that the word 'God' has become unusable. Silence about God is therefore not the consequence of linguistic analysis, but an axiom that van Buren has introduced for other reasons. I would suggest, however, that this is not an axiom, but rather that the necessity of preserving silence about God is connected with a pollution in van Buren's thought of the method of linguistic analysis with the verification principle as formulated in an earlier stage of logical positivism.

Finally, what is faith and how ought the language of faith to be understood? Van Buren uses two words which he has borrowed from Ian T. Ramsey to answer this question— 'discernment' and 'commitment'. By discernment, we perceive (anew) the Reality in the absolute certainty that 'this is it' and this discernment, which the disciples, for example, had on the day of Christ's resurrection, is closely linked with 'commitment', our taking the risk of accepting that this is really 'it'.

The language of faith is therefore a language which bears witness to this discernment and the commitment which is associated with it. The Bible cannot be read simply as information about facts—about the fact, for instance, that on a certain day a grave that had been closed with a stone was found empty—but as the text in which the apostles express their discernment and their commitment. We can only read the Bible as historical information if we completely misunderstand the character and the logical structure of the language game that is played in the Bible!

Thus van Buren ends up very near to Bultmann. His interpretation of the gospel is 'certainly close to the existentialist-theological interpretation . . . but an important difference is evident in the fact that the history of Jesus of Nazareth is central in and integral to it.'[1] It is in this history that the freedom which henceforth and for all time determines the historical perspective of faith is experienced.

[1] *Op. cit.,* 171.

CARL MICHALSON

ALTHOUGH Paul van Buren is influenced by Bultmann, he is even more influenced by Bonhoeffer, and the effect that *Letters and Papers from Prison* has had in America can also be seen in the work of Carl Michalson. I shall confine myself here to Michalson's latest publication, *The Rationality of Faith*. This book is not a dogmatic theology, setting out the teaching of the Church, but a methodological study of the kind that is found in the so-called Prolegomena of dogmatics. Philosophy plays an even more important part in Michalson's theological thought than in van Buren's but in the case of Michalson, it is not so much the philosophy of linguistic analysis as that of Kierkegaard and especially the phenomenology of E. Husserl, M. Heidegger, J. P. Sartre and M. Merleau-Ponty, which throws light on the intentionality of the human consciousness and the structure of history and authentic human historicity.

Leaving aside a number of methodological considerations which take up a great deal of space in Michalson's book, it is noteworthy that the author describes Christian faith at the end of his book as 'historical maturity', a formula which is directly traceable to one of Bonhoeffer's leading themes in *Letters and Papers from Prison*.

Living in history, man looks for a meaning which will throw light on his life. The meaning which he finds or which he looks for without finding is not his own creation, nor can it be found 'objectively' in facts. It comes from his encounter with others in the tradition—Hegel's 'objective spirit'—from which men live. But the meaning that man looks for and for which he risks his life—this meaning is such that it has to be lived and that human life is risked for it—is always being assailed. We live all the time on the verge of the 'historicity' that is expressed in modern literature—the fatal conclusion that life has no meaning and that we are living for nothing.

The gospel enters this situation of historicity. Whenever it is accepted in faith, life gains its definitive meaning and historicity is permanently overcome. 'History for the Christian is the interworld of meaning constituted by events which embrace God's word to man and man's obedient response.'[1] Michalson's use of the word 'interworld' indicates that meaning is not imposed on the world by men and is not to be found in 'facts' themselves, but that it can only come about in an encounter in which man risks himself.

Christian faith is eschatological. This does not mean that faith is on the way towards the end, living in the expectation of future events, the *eschata* or 'last things'. It means that Christians live out in the present the definitive meaning that God has given to life. 'Biblical eschatology (rather) deals with *eschaton*, the last, the ultimate, the final reality, reality as an attribute of God's being present.'[2] It is with this *eschaton* that love, patience, simplicity, joy and, in all this, freedom and historical responsibility enter human life.

Thus men live 'eschatologically'—the word is reminiscent of Bultmann—within the sphere of history and without 'ends beyond history', because 'Christianity is not a preparation for life after death, for it is a candid admission that we know nothing of such a future except that God is in it.'[3] This living on this side of the grave which we have found in Bonhoeffer and in Paul van Buren and which we shall also encounter in Harvey E. Cox characterizes Michalson's interpretation of Christian faith.

Christians, then, live out their faith in the history of this world and are responsible for what becomes of the world. This is the essence of Christian faith—not that God, as the all-powerful 'controller' governs the world and sees to it that his will is done whatever men may do, but rather that he has entrusted the world to men or, to put it even more strongly, that he has handed it over to men. The essence of the gospel is contained in Paul's statements in his letter to the Galatians: 'You are no longer a slave but a son' (*Gal.* 4: 7) and in his

[1]C. Michalson, *The Rationality of Faith*, London 1964, 105.
[2]*Ibid.* 137.
[3]*Ibid.* 138.

first epistle to the Corinthians: 'All things are yours' (1 *Cor.* 3: 21). This, and nothing else, is grace and it is in this sense that what Thérèse de Lisieux said is true: 'Tout est grâce'. Grace is our being able to live in an authentic historical responsibility. We can no longer fall back on a God who will see to it that everything will be all right. We can no longer withdraw from history. On the contrary, we are made capable of living in time in love, patience, simplicity and so on and above all in genuine responsibility. This is ultimately and really *your* life. As soon as this has been said, we find ourselves confronted with one of the main themes of the theology of the death of God.

All this has clear consequences for the Church, the eschatological community on earth. Her task is not to call men away from history to 'ends beyond history', but to make them responsible for the world so that peace is established there, reconciliation is achieved and men live in the world in simplicity and joy. She must not disparage the coming of age and the maturity which God has given to men and she must realize that she does not exist for herself, but for the world and that God is not concerned with the Church, but with the world. She must understand that she is not the aim, but an instrument—and an interim and she must be conscious of the fact that she will disappear when mankind has (at last) learnt to live in historical responsibility. Whereas Marxists look forward to a future without a state, Christians look forward to a future without a Church. Both look forward to the freedom, meaning and horizon of history.

GIBSON WINTER

BUT where is the Church? According to Gibson Winter, Professor of Ethics and Society in the Theological Faculty of the University of Chicago, the Church is absent in America. There are, of course, Churches in America which are much more 'in' than the Churches in Europe and there are frequent 'revivals' of colossal proportions, like those of Billy Graham.

There is a lot of 'religion' and, from the statistical point of view, the United States is probably the most Christian country in the world. But the Church is absent and, in the battle for the future and for a more human society, the voice of the Churches is scarcely audible. They are confined to the suburbs of the great cities where the American looks for a place of peace and security in the struggle for existence. It is in, suburbia that the Churches are present, an element of peace and tranquillity in a world that is too great to be taken in and what they offer men is a feeling of continuity and security—in a word, opium. Winter never uses Marx's word explicitly, but he is not far from Marx in his characterization of the situation with the word *amnesia,* or loss of memory. In the suburbs, one can (among one's equals) forget—one can forget the past and the future, injustice and conflict. The Churches help one to forget and give one reassurance. You are 'accepted'. Everything is all right. They contribute to the plot against responsibility for the *res publica* that is hatched in this world. And in the meantime the Churches, the opium-dens, are absent from those places where the future is made and unmade in the harsh struggle for a new mankind. This dark picture, which is, at first sight, so much in contradiction with statistics, is fully supported by American sociologists such as Peter L. Berger (in, for example, an ironical book, *The Noise of Solemn Assemblies*). There are churches in America, but there is no Church.

After this diagnosis, we come to such very elementary questions as what is proclaiming the gospel, what is faith, what is the Church and how can the new creation that Paul talks about (2 *Cor.* 5: 17) be given a form in the metropolis that is growing up around us? Or is all this impossible, and are we bound to conclude, as Friedrich Naumann has done, that the gospel of the carpenter from Nazareth has nothing to say to us in our urban environment of the twentieth century and the technological world?

The New Creation as Metropolis is mainly concerned with ecclesiology, with what a Church is and with the task of a

Church in the world. When he comes to answer this question, Winter turns to Bonhoeffer; Bonhoeffer again—the man who found the symbol of faith and the Church in Isaiah 53, in the canticles of the Servant of Yahweh and who reproached the Churches of his own time, and in particular the Confessing Church of Germany, for having withdrawn from the world into a position of self-defence, when the Church is either there for the world or else is not there at all. Armed with Bonhoeffer's facts, Winter sketches a picture of the 'Servant Church' and of faith as 'servanthood' to God and thus to men in those places where the battle must be waged against the powers and structures that bar the way to a more human society—where the Churches say that it is impossible!

What does this service consist of? It is not hard to guess. The American longing, the American dream is to forget, to cease to think—*amnesia*. The Church's duty, then, is *anamnēsis*. This word can be found in the New Testament in the context of the institution of the Last Supper and it is usually translated by 'commemoration'. It is also used in psychiatry, in connection with the process of bringing to consciousness what has been thrust into the unconscious. *Anamnēsis*, the first great task of the Church, is the process of making men conscious of the authentic issues and of their authentic responsibilities as men who have a future which is in their hands and in no one else's.

Thus the Church can be described as the prophetic community which wages war—as the prophets did in the Old Testament—for humanity and human communication and against everything that stands in the way of a human future, including the treacherous religiosity which refuses to take part in this conflict and avoids it. It is therefore not surprising that Winter, like Paul van Buren, should use the word 'commitment'. In his case, it is a commitment to the things of this world, to the racial problem, the war in Vietnam, equal rights, poverty and wealth, social justice and so on.

In contrast to the hitherto existing Churches, Gibson Winter's Church is a Church of laypeople, a Church of the *laos* (that is, the Greek 'people'), of the people of God in the world. They carry the apostolate out into the world, the metropolis. They are called from amnesia to keep historical reflection alive in a world of anxiety, self-preservation, striving for power and the self-stupefaction of a matriarchal environment. They are vigilant in prophesying the future in the light of the Bible. Once again, we are reminded of what Pascal once said—as we were in the case of Bonhoeffer—'Jesus will be in agony until the end of the world. We must not be asleep during that time.'

Not much is left in the theology of Gibson Winter of the security that the Church, the mother of the faithful, offered to her children in past ages. The very opposite is the case—Christians are called to take on themselves their responsibility for the future of mankind, to embody it in their lives and to live with it and with others, unprotected, in history. They will often find that their allies in this struggle are not members of the religious organizations at all, but are in the ranks of non-Christians, since there is a hidden Church—a theme that occurs in the writings of Paul Tillich—a latent Church that is closer to the kingdom of God than the Churches themselves. The difference between Christians and non-Christians, then, is that, for Christians, humanity—and it is with *men* and only men that history is concerned—has, once and for all time, been defined in the tradition that is concerned with Jesus the messiah, the anointed one.

Where, then, is the missionary territory of the Church in this situation? The answer is quite clear—it is the world, the metropolis. But something else has to be said before this answer is given—the missionary territory of the Church is the Churches! The *anamnēsis* of the gospel has to do its work first in the Churches, so that they can take their place in the *polis*.

HARVEY E. COX

A KIND of sequence can be observed in recent American theology. The same themes can be heard again and again—

they may be slightly changed or in a different key, but they are clearly recognizable. And always there is Bonhoeffer, with his letters and notes, in the background. This is also the case in *The Secular City* by Harvey E. Cox who, until recently, was Associate Professor for Church and Society at the University of Harvard (Theological Faculty). This book, which also deals with the future of secularized society—called by Cox not the metropolis, but the technopolis—was quickly acclaimed in Europe after its first publication in the United States.

We have already seen how Cox characterized the 'secular city' and how he made a connection between secularization and the proclamation of the gospel in the history of the West. I shall have to leave out much of what he says in his book here and confine myself simply to what he has to say about the Church. Cox believes that the Church has to appear in the world as an exorcist. In the ancient world, an exorcist was one who engaged in a struggle with demons and spirits and with cases of human possession by demons. Exorcism occurs in the New Testament (in *Acts* 19: 13, for example) and, among other things, Jesus himself was also an exorcist. With the disappearance of the ancient world-view, this exorcism also disappeared in a world that no longer acknowledged demons and possession by demons. But, in the modern world too, men are at the mercy of powers which deprive them of their humanity. These principalities and powers of our own times are those things which are taken for granted and not critically examined, the 'social myths', the ideologies which lay down in advance how life must be lived. Cox could also have pointed to Heidegger's anonymous dictatorship of 'one', except that he has nothing to say in favour of Heidegger! For Cox, then, exorcism is unmasking and contesting these principalities and powers in our own society, powers which threaten men's lives and deprive them of the possibility of living as human beings. In this world, the Church, unmasking and at the same time placing herself *de facto* in the tradition of salvation, bears witness to the freedom which God gives

us and which only he can give us. Cox does not offer us any
'ends beyond history', but he does present us with a struggle
for the future *polis* of freedom and *šālôm* (peace) on this
earth. The Church is the 'avant-garde' of this future *polis* on
earth and the sign that points, not to the *Civitas Dei,* but to
the 'City of Man'.

Anyone wishing to think about the Church must begin
with the world, in other words, with history and with the
political decisions which make or mar the future. Harvey
Cox shares this view with Gibson Winter. The world is, after
all, the sphere in which God does his work, freeing and renewing. God is not interested in the Church and in religion
—he is interested in the world and in politics. He is to be
found wherever civilizations collide, wherever attacks are
risked against the structures of power in the *polis* and against
the injustice that is built into these structures. He is to be
found wherever men reject the traditional norms of religion
and ethics in order to be with God in everything that he is
doing in the world. He is to be found in the revolution in
which the old world is destroyed.

We must not, in Cox's view, think of God as the Almighty
living in heaven, but as the God who goes ahead of us in the
revolutionary events of history and calls us to follow him.
Much of what Cox says in this context is reminiscent of
Bonhoeffer, and this is certainly the case when he says that
theologians of our own time must devote themselves more to
the struggle against the spiritualization of the Bible than to
demythologization. This, he says, can best be done by standing with one foot in the Old Testament and the other in the
political struggle of our world, for the man who has taken
up his position thus is capable of finding out what God has
to say in the New Testament to men of the present age.

It is only when we have been through this revolution in our
own thinking and no longer think about the world from the
vantage-point of the Church, but think about the Church
from the vantage-point of the world, that we shall be able to
ask ourselves not what the Church is, but what the Church's

task is in God's revolution which is taking place in this world. 'Ministry' is, after all, being at work with God in his world—in his revolution.

Can we still speak about God? The question is reminiscent of Bonhoeffer in his letter of 30 April 1944, when he asked how we could speak, if we could still 'speak' at all as we had been able to up till then, in a secular way about God. If we are still to speak about God, then we must certainly do so 'in a secular way', in other words, not in a religious way, but in a way that is related to the revolutionary developments in the world of our own times. But is it still possible? Cox knows and acknowledges that, for most people, the word 'God' has become an empty word that arouses no response at all. '. . . it may well be that our English word God will have to die, corroborating in some measure Nietzsche's apocalyptic judgement that "God is dead".'[1] Yet Christianity is unlike Buddhism, for example—it must speak about God and cannot take refuge in silence. The only possible course, then, is to point with the word 'God' to a reality which crosses our path in this world, in the people and especially in the revolutionary events of our own age. God is not a 'He' who can be described. There is a power that imposes itself and a voice that calls. There is a name, a name that we give. But this name cannot be said in any place where everything is motionless and where things remain as they are, because God is not there.

[1]H. Cox, *The Secular City*, S.C.M. Press, London 1966, 265.

The Death of God

BIBLIOGRAPHY

APART from a single note in the writings of Pascal, the theme of the death of God first occurred in European literature in Jean Paul Richter's discourse of the dead Christ in his novel *Siebenkäs*, the 'Rede des toten Christus vom Weltgebäude herab, das kein Gott sei' (see Jean Paul, *Werke II*, Munich, 1959). The theme recurred later, in a very different key, in the work of Hölderlin.

In nineteenth-century philosophy, it can be found in G. W. F. Hegel (see Roger Garaudy's excellent, but difficult study, *Dieu est mort. Etude sur Hegel*, Paris, 1962), in Karl Marx and, above all, in Friedrich Nietzsche. Nietzsche's most important writings in this connection will be found in *Die fröhliche Wissenschaft*, fragment 125 and especially fragment 343 and in *Also sprach Zarathustra* (see Friedrich Nietzsche, *Werke*, edited by Karl Schlechta, Volume II, Carl Hanser Verlag, Munich, pp. 126–8, 205–6, 278–81, 497–501, 501–5). A great deal has been written about the death of God in Nietzsche's philosophy. One of the most interesting of these studies is Martin Heidegger's essay, 'Nietzsches Wort "Gott ist tot"' in the collection *Holzwege*, published by Vittorio Klostermann, Frankfurt a.M., 1950, pp. 193–247.

The theme of the death of God first occurred in American theology in Gabriel Vahanian's book, *The Death of God. The Culture of our Post-Christian Era*, which was published in 1961 by Braziller of New York. A second book by Vahanian was also published by Braziller of New York in 1964. This was

entitled *Wait without Idols*. Vahanian's books, which are inspired by Karl Barth, Dietrich Bonhoeffer and especially
Sören Kierkegaard, are an attack on the 'religious establishment' in America. He attacks the Churches because they
obscure the reality of the living God and thus preserve an
illusion—the illusion that, in 'Christianity', we still have to
do with the living God. Vahanian analyses not the death of
God, but modern man's inability still to believe in God. He is
therefore far removed from William Hamilton and Thomas
J. J. Altizer, who are the leading exponents of the 'death of
God' theology.

William Hamilton's book, *The New Essence of Christianity*,
was published in 1961 by the Association Press of New York.
In the second chapter of this book, he discusses the 'death of
God' and the possibility of (Christian) faith in the period of
his death.

In 1966, Thomas J. J. Altizer's book, *The Gospel of Christian
Atheism*, was published by the Westminster Press of Philadelphia. It is clear from this book that Hamilton and Altizer have
little more in common than the theme of the death of God.

In 1968, *Radical Theology and the Death of God*, a collection
dedicated to the memory of Paul Tillich and consisting of
essays written by both William Hamilton and Thomas
Altizer between 1963 and 1966 and including one earlier
essay on Dostoievski written by Hamilton in 1959, was
published by Pelican Books.

Part of the discussion stimulated by the 'radical theology'
can be found in *The Death of God Debate*, a book compiled by
Jackson Lee Ice and John J. Carey and published in 1967 by
the Westminster Press of Philadelphia. This book includes a
number of criticisms of the 'radical theology'—one of them
was written by Gabriel Vahanian—and Hamilton's and
Altizer's replies to these criticisms.

A good account of this theology will be found in the
American theologian Thomas W. Ogletree's book, *The 'Death
of God' Controversy* (SCM Press, London, 1966).

Dorothee Sölle must also be mentioned in connection with

the 'radical theology'—the subtitle to her book *Stellvertretung* (Kreuz Verlag, Stuttgart and Berlin, 1965), is, after all, *Ein Kapitel Theologie nach dem Tode Gottes*. In 1967, Helmut Gollwitzer's detailed criticism of Dorothee Sölle's book, *Von der Stellvertretung Gottes. Christlicher Glaube in der Erfahrung de Verborgenheit Gottes*, was published in Germany. Dorothee Sölle writes about the death of God; Gollwitzer, on the other hand, discusses his concealment (*Verborgenheit*). According to the title page, Gollwitzer wrote this book as a contribution to the 'dialogue with Dorothee Sölle', but criticism such as Gollwitzer's leaves little scope for the dialogue that ought to follow.

A number of Dorothee Sölle's lectures were published in book form with the title *Die Wahrheit ist konkret* in 1967, that is, after the appearance of *Stellvertretung*, by Walter Verlag of Olten and Freiburg. Most of these lectures were, however, given before *Stellvertretung* was written. Seven of the ten date back to the period between 1960 and 1962 and only the last, 'Kirche ausserhalb der Kirche', was given in 1965. They therefore represent an earlier stage in Dorothee Sölle's thought and show that the course that she has followed began with Rudolf Bultmann and his *Existenzialinterpretation* of Scripture. The text of the lecture 'Kirche ausserhalb der Kirche' is almost exactly the same as that of the speech made by Dorothee Sölle at the Church Convention of 1965. This speech, which has the same title as the lecture, was published separately in 1965.

In *Radical Theology and the Death of God*, Hamilton had this to say of the 'radical theologians'.

A number of names are given to this fourth group, none of which is entirely satisfactory. One hears of the 'new' theology, the secular, the radical, the death of God theology. I think radical is perfectly adequate, though there is often a kind of arrogance in ascribing this to oneself . . . The name I prefer for theological radicalism is the death of God theology.

The death of God radical theologians, recently given far more visibility than they either desired or deserved, are men without God who do not anticipate his return. But it is not a simple not-having, for there is an experience of loss. Painful for some, not so for others, it is loss none the less. The loss is not of the idols, or of the God of theism, but of the God of the Christian tradition. And this group persists, in the face of both bewilderment and fury, in calling itself Christian. It persists in making use of the phrase 'death of God', in spite of its rhetorical colour, partly because it is a phrase that cannot be adapted to traditional use by the theologians today.

What is the relation of radical theology to the Church? It certainly must be clear that this theology has neither the power nor the ability to serve the Protestant Church in most of its present institutional forms. I do not see how preaching, worship, prayer, ordination, the sacraments can be taken seriously by the radical theologian. If there is a need for new institutional forms and styles, however, this theology doubtless has a great deal to say. If theology is tested by its ability to shape new kinds of personal and corporate existence in the times in which it lives, then it would seem that radical theology may be able to pass such a test.[1]

We may deduce from what Hamilton wrote that the radical theology aims to break with the whole of 'Christianity'. It is not the idols that are dead and not the God of theism—that had already been said by Tillich, Bultmann, Bonhoeffer, van Buren and many others!—but the God of the Christian tradition. Nonetheless, Hamilton and Altizer still call themselves Christian theologians, and rightly so, because they have made it their task to express what Christian faith in the period of the death of God can be.

Even though the radical theology is dominated by a break

[1]T. Altizer and W. Hamilton, *Radical Theology and the Death of God*, London 1968, 21–2.

with the past, there is nonetheless a certain continuity with that past. Langdon Gilkey has mapped out relationships between the radical theology and Karl Barth, Paul Tillich and Rudolf Bultmann. He could certainly have mentioned Bonhoeffer in this context. For Hamilton at least, the way which was to lead him from Karl Barth to the radical theology began with the reading of translations of fragments of Bonhoeffer's *Letters and Papers*. And in addition to these twentieth-century theologians, there are also the nineteenth-century philosophers—Nietzsche, of course, and, in the case of Altizer, also Hegel, Kierkegaard and the apocalyptic poet William Blake. Dorothee Sölle too was decisively inspired by Hegel in her theology, 'after the death of God'.

What do these theologians mean, then, by the death of God? Are they speaking about modern man's experience that God—once the *ens realissimum*, the most real being in the whole of reality—is no longer experienced? Yes, they are certainly speaking about this—they are, as Hamilton has said, not discussing the absence of the experience of God, but the experience of his absence. But there is more to it than this. Are they speaking about the world and saying that the world—once a 'beautiful book', in which God was to be read —no longer allows God to be seen? Yes, they are, but there is even more to it than just this. In speaking about the death of God, people are not simply speaking about themselves and about the world—they really intend to say something about God, not about the idols and the God of theism, but about God the Father, the Almighty, the creator of heaven and earth. Again, as Hamilton has said, the present of the radical theologians is similar to that of the atheists, but they have different memories of the past. This atheism goes further than that of Tillich, Robinson or van Buren. As a result, more is required than simply a new reformation.

We must try to map out the possible meanings of the formula 'God is dead'. What we shall discover is that these meanings overlap to such an extent that no clear picture will emerge.

The formula points firstly to the need for iconoclasm, an act which will not result in the killing of God himself, but of his image or images. The images that we make of God remove God from our sight and alienate us from him. They form a wall, an iconostasis, between man and God and they must therefore be smashed. The image of God created by the wisdom of the Jews was broken in this way in Job's conversations with his friends and, in the same way, the image of God formed by classical theology that survived up to the time of Hegel and Nietzsche, has also been destroyed in our own period. In this case, however, it is more a question of the death of the images of God than of the death of God himself, who outlives all his images.

The formula 'God is dead' can also express the conviction, stated by Ludwig Feuerbach and Karl Marx and—once again—by Friedrich Nietzsche, that all our speaking about God is 'theopoesie' (to use Feuerbach's word), in other words, that men make God after their own image and likeness. This is, of course, the very opposite to what is said about God and men in Genesis 1 : 26. Anthropology has therefore to provide the solution to theology and the anthropological structure or the socio-political configuration of which 'God' is the exponent has to be brought to light. If this is done, God is placed, as an independent reality, outside man and, in contrast to him, he is dead.

'God is dead' can also be the symbol of a situation in which man is fully responsible for the world and for the future. This is the situation which Harvey E. Cox has described with the words: 'The world has become the task and the responsibility of man'. We can no longer count on God intervening at the moment when men fail. This God—the god of religion, as Bonhoeffer would say—is dead and it is no longer possible for us to go back to the land of childhood where a loving Father cares for us.

Finally, the formula can refer to a new form and experience of the Christian faith in a post-theist period, and it is in this sense that it is used above all in the 'death of God' theology.

10

God was there, but he is there no longer. He is dead. This death is not the end of the Christian faith, but it is certainly the end of traditional Christianity. In the future, and even now, in the present, Christian faith is and will be something quite different from what it has been hitherto. And there is no way back.

It is especially this last meaning that is expressed in the formula, 'God is dead'. The situation is not one of God being silent though soon he will speak again. It is not one of God being absent though he will soon come back again. It is not one of the 'darkness of God' though it will soon be light again. The situation is one of the death of God who was not and will not come back. The God who will soon speak—presently, when it is light again—will be a different one from the God of traditional metaphysical and religious Christianity. The situation of the death of God is the situation of Hölderlin in the nineteenth century and that of Heidegger in the twentieth.

The theology of the death of God tries to say—in this new situation!—what Christian faith is and what the 'new essence of Christianity' (the title of William Hamilton's book) consists of. The theologians of the death of God, then, are attempting to define this new essence of Christianity because there is, in their opinion, no continuity with Christianity of the past which would make it possible to speak about the essence of Christianity as Adolf von Harnack did and as Robinson has done in describing our new situation in terms of a new reformation.

All this can be deduced from the texts, but no more than this. It is not a clear picture, but I cannot make it any clearer. It would seem that these theologians have seized hold of Nietzsche's words because we still lack a language that can adequately express our present situation. Language is orientated towards the past, but the experience is that of the present. There is a distance between language and existence. In Heidegger's words, we are 'on the way towards language'. The reality slips through between the words of our language.

We say 'God is dead', but we do not know what we are saying.

The death of God—when did it happen? Various answers are possible. We may say, as Altizer has done, that it took place when God left heaven in Christ and came down to earth. Or we may say that it happened when Jesus was crucified and darkness came over the whole land. Or we may say that it took place in the nineteenth century, between the French Revolution and the Second World War. Nietzsche called the death of God the 'greatest modern event' and noted in this context that an event of this kind requires time before it reaches people. Or we may even say that the death of God occurs at the moment when men experience that

> heaven is mute and mute and mute and so on
>
> Hans Andreus.

It is only when one comprehensive answer has been reached, including all these answers, that an adequate answer will have been found.

We have seen that Altizer and Dorothee Sölle (in whose case we can more properly speak, not of the death of God, but of his absence) are partly influenced in their thought by Hegel, with the result that the death of God in their case (not in the case of Hamilton) is a dialectical theme—death is an aspect in God's being. God is dead, certainly, and he is dead in our time, in our lives and in our history, but presently he will be 'everything to every one' (1 *Cor.* 15: 28). Is this God of the future, this eschatological God, the same God as the God of the past? Here too, the answer is dialectical. The God of the future, whom we do not yet know, is a different God from the God of the past. He is not a God out there beyond the stars. He is not a God who is transcendent and lonely. He is a God who happens in the world. And yet he is the same God. God only seems to be undialectically dead in the case of Hamilton, whose theology therefore presents us with the greatest enigmas, although at first sight it would appear to be the most simple.

WILLIAM HAMILTON

THE world of the nineteen-thirties was the world of existentialism, of Eliot's Prufrock and of Bessie Smith's Empty-Bed Blues. The world of the nineteen-sixties is that of the Beatles, of A Hard Day's Night and of We Shall Overcome. We are living in a period of new optimism. We are able to change the world and we shall not fail to change it. All that is said about sin and estrangement may well be true, but we are not impotent in our confrontation with this world. One of the themes of this new optimism is the death of God. We must ourselves do what we previously entrusted to God. We must not pray for our neighbour—we must be with him in the struggle for bread and space, for freedom and the future, in the imitation of Christ. For Hamilton, the theology of the death of God is a theology of the imitation of Christ in this world.

A clear development is discernible in Hamilton's thought. He began with Karl Barth, but Bonhoeffer's *Letters and Papers* and questions of the theodicy—expressed by Dostoievski in *The Brothers Karamazov* and by Albert Camus in *The Plague*—alienated him from this beginning. It was in his *New Essence of Christianity* that Hamilton first wrote about the death of God, but here it was more a question of God's absence—Hamilton was waiting for the absent one and faith was hope of his return. At a later stage, he considered the possible meaning of what Augustine had to say about the *frui Deo*, the 'enjoyment' of God. At a still later stage, God was, for him, really dead. What distinguishes the radical theologian from the atheist, then, is not that he has a different future, but that he lives with different memories. To the question as to how we must imagine that the God who was once alive and was indeed life itself is now dead—note, however, that Hamilton is not talking here about himself and not about the world, but really about God!—Hamilton gives no answer.

Hamilton the atheist is a Christian and a theologian. This is possible because, while God is dead, Jesus is the Lord of our lives. This Lord is not the God-man of the Christological dogma, but Jesus of Nazareth as we encounter him in the New Testament. In this connection, Hamilton refers to the conclusion of Albert Schweitzer's great book on the history of historical research into the life of Jesus. Jesus comes to us, says Hamilton, as an unknown and nameless one, as he once came, at the edge of the lake, to the men who did not know who he was. And he says the same: 'Follow me!' . . . He commands and to those who obey him he will reveal himself in everything that they may experience in communion with him in the way of peace and conflict and sorrow. Christ is in the world, in people, in *this* struggle for right and in *that* fight for clarity and order, but he is, as it were, masked. Our task is to unmask him, to stay with him and to do his work. Even if the radical theologian does not know what he must believe, he does know where he has to be. His reality is not that of faith, nor that of hope, but that of love. His place is not in the Church, but in the world, or rather, the Church is there where Christ takes shape among people in the world.

This means that the Church can disappear as an independent institution alongside the world. At the time of the Reformation, Christianity began to move out of the monastery towards the world. This was the beginning of the secularization of Christianity, but only a beginning. The movement has not yet been completed. For centuries, Christianity continued to live in heteronomous and hierarchical structures and the Christian faith remained a religion in Bonhoeffer's sense. We have the task of going to the end of the road, of forsaking the Church of the past and, in the struggle for the future, of finding new forms of community which will no longer be exclusively Christian, but will be orientated towards Christ's rule and the coming of his kingdom.

In one of his most recent writings, Hamilton outlines the most important tasks of the radical theology in the immediate future. Work must be done on Christology—the traditional Christology will have to give way to or be linked with an approach that is dominated by the imitation of Christ. Work must also be done on anthropology—the word 'sin' has to be re-defined now that it no longer refers to man's relationship with God, and the new optimism must be given an anthropological basis. Work must also be done on ecclesiology and especially on the problem of the meaning of the Church, the ecclesiastical offices and the sacraments within the framework of the radical theology, which has forsaken the Churches. There must be dialogue with the Jews—believers and non-believers—and with the other atheistic religion, Buddhism. Finally, a new study must be made of the nineteenth century, because the nineteenth century is to the radical theology what the sixteenth century was to Karl Barth, and Hamilton insists that we need an entirely different nineteenth century from the one that traditional Protestant theology has left us.

There are considerable differences between Hamilton and Harvey Cox, especially in the question of the death of God, and, in *Playboy*, Cox emphatically dissociated himself from the theology of the death of God. There is, however, one thing about which they are agreed—the need for Christians to play an active part in the revolution in which men are looking for the way to the city of man. Both Hamilton and Cox have come to this conclusion by reflecting about Bonhoeffer's letters. But Hamilton goes farther along the way indicated by these letters—the dualism of Church and world has entirely disappeared in his case. In this, he certainly goes farther than Bonhoeffer intended.

THOMAS ALTIZER

THERE are also great differences between Hamilton and Altizer, even purely formally. Whereas Hamilton's thought is fragmentary and he will not say any more than can be said, Altizer tries to obtain a vision of reality as a whole in the power of his thought. And whereas what Hamilton has written is at first sight completely translucent, everything that Altizer has written so far is obscure and difficult to understand. It is the language of a visionary who is not always able to grasp what he sees, full of William Blake's apocalyptic symbols and Hegel's dialectics.

Altizer's path began with Paul Tillich and it was probably he who was responsible for the dedication of the collection, *Radical Theology and the Death of God,* to the memory of Tillich. Among the theologians of the twentieth century, wrote Altizer, only Tillich had pointed a way to a really contemporary theology. Wherever he had to reject Tillich's conclusions and oppose them, he did so in the certainty that they were still not radical enough and thinking of his own words, that the real Tillich was the radical Tillich. This first encounter with theology was followed by a study of the history of religion under Mircea Eliade. Then Nietzsche came within his orbit, then Hegel and finally William Blake. With these stones, which are different from those used by Hamilton, Altizer fashioned his variation on the theology of the death of God.

Hamilton is a man who feels at home in modern America and who has confidence in the future. Altizer, on the other hand, is a man who beats himself defencelessly against the void, the estrangement and the dehumanization of America today. His greatest temptation, then, is not to easy optimism, but rather to that resentment which so preoccupied Nietzsche and to a gnostic exodus from the world—but to where? To nowhere, because there is nothing outside this world. The transcendent being, the God of Christianity, is dead.

The death of God is not something that we must mourn as the disciples mourned on the way to Emmaus because their master had been crucified, 'but we had hoped . . . ' (*Luke* 24:21). With Robinson, we are at the end of theism and faced with the question as to whether it is possible to live in the modern age and not be an atheist on the way to Emmaus. This is not the case with Altizer. His book is called the 'gospel' of the death of God! It is a gospel because, with the death of the stranger with whom man has always found himself confronted, the way has been opened to the 'Great Humanity

Divine' of William Blake, to the ultimate unity of God with men, the goal of history. It is a gospel too because God has not been 'superseded' by death, but because he annihilated himself as the transcendent stranger when he left heaven in Christ, came down to earth and carried the cross to Golgotha. It is also a gospel because

> if God dieth not for Man and giveth not himself
> Eternally for Man, Man could not exist . . .
> William Blake.

The great visionaries of the nineteenth century—Blake, Hegel and Nietzsche—were the first to understand the gospel of the death of God. They did not therefore accept the death of God reluctantly—they willed his death. We must follow them today. We consequently have nothing to look for in the past, not even in the Christianity of the past. Nor have we anything to expect from the present, which is void, desert, darkness, estrangement and dehumanization. At the most, we can only suffer and endure. Altizer's gaze is turned towards the future. Christian faith is the eschatological expectation of the kingdom or of the *coincidentia oppositorum*.

The coincidence of opposites is the great symbol of Altizer's theology. This symbol is taken from the mystical philosophy of Nicholas of Cusa, but Hegel's philosophy is also a philosophy of the coincidence of opposites in which, unlike that of Nicholas, history has also been given a place. In the case of Altizer, the opposites are—and here Mircea Eliade plays a part—the sacral and the profane, or God and the 'world', but this is already an interpretation which Eliade would oppose. The whole of history is a way towards the coincidence of opposites through the dialectical contrast of the sacral and the profane since God annihilated himself when he came as Christ. God is not. He is becoming, or rather, he will be. Man is history and God is also history and both are on the way towards the coincidence of opposites in which God will be 'everything to every one' (1 *Cor.* 15:28). It is also possible to

say that both are on the way towards their identity. But before
the sacral and the profane coincide in the 'Great Humanity
Divine', they will have to diverge still more. The profane will
have to become emptier and more profane, but without our
forsaking it in resentment, just as for Marx (Altizer does not
himself make this comparison, but it would seem to be
obvious) the opposites in the class war have to become even
more pronounced before the coincidence of opposites of the
classless society becomes a fact. Anyone who withdraws from
the dialectics of history by holding on to the past or by seeking
the salvation of the future in the past, as Christianity always
did before Blake and Hegel, and as a rule still does, stands in
the way of salvation and the kingdom.

But what does taking part in the dynamism of history mean
in the context of the social and political dilemmas of our own
times? To this question, Altizer does not give any satisfactory
answer. All that he gives us is the scornful observation that
nothing has happened—however horrible things may appear
—or, if anything has happened, the theologians of 'God' have
approved of it. We must break with Christianity and we may
not go back to the past. But what does this mean? Hamilton
is certainly clearer here than Altizer.

DOROTHEE SÖLLE

THERE is much that reminds us of Altizer in the most
remarkable document produced in Europe on the theology
of the death of God—Dorothee Sölle's *Stellvertretung* (*Representation*), sub-titled as a *Theology After the Death of God*. I am
thinking in this connection especially of the theme of the God
who is still on the way towards himself, who *is* not, but will
be. The difference between Dorothee Sölle and Thomas
Altizer is, among other things, to be found in the fact that
she has looked for a stronger connection with theological
tradition and that she is concerned, in her thinking, with the
question asked by Bonhoeffer, 'who Christ really is for us
to-day'. *Stellvertretung* might therefore be called an attempted

religionless interpretation of Christology in which—as distinct from Bonhoeffer—Hegel and the theme of the death of God have been given a place. There is no sign in *Stellvertretung* of any familiarity on the part of the writer with the radical theology of America and, on their part, Hamilton and Altizer are silent about this European theology after the death of God.

Dorothee Sölle characterizes the period in which we are living with such words as post-metaphysical, post-religious and post-theist and she uses these words more or less synonymously. She does not agree with Bonhoeffer that we are approaching a religionless period, but believes that, even in the future, religion will continue, both inside and outside Christianity, as a foreign and atavistic element in a new world. The formula 'God is dead' thus refers in her book to the God of theism. This God, 'more certain than the personal ego', is no longer there and nothing points to him. If God is still there, in our world, then he is no longer there as the Father 'out there beyond the stars', but incognito, in the form of 'the least of these my brethren' (*Matt.* 25:40), so that a direct relationship with God, like that of the mystical union or that of prayer, is no longer possible. These are, of course, themes that we have already encountered in Bonhoeffer and Bonhoeffer's voice can be heard quite clearly in several passages of *Stellvertretung*.

In this new situation, Dorothee Sölle's question is 'who Christ really is, for us to-day'—Bonhoeffer's question, in other words. What is surprising, however, is that Dorothee Sölle answers this question with a very old theme in Christian theology that has become marginal since the Enlightenment —the theme of Christ as the 'representative' (*der Stellvertreter*), who replaces or takes the place of men—men who are absent! —with God and who replaces God—the God who is absent —with men. It should be remembered, however, that there is a fundamental difference between the substitute or replacer (*der Ersatzmann*) who permanently takes the other's place (so that the other is eliminated, without future and *dead*) and the one who provisionally and temporarily replaces the other, waiting for his coming. Christ, then, is not, in Dorothee Sölle's book, the permanent replacer of the dead God of the past, but the temporary representative of the future, the living God and, together with Robinson and van Buren, she refers to John 14:9, the text which, in Robinson's opinion, is to be as fundamental to the new reformation as Romans 1:17 was for Luther. But anyone who aims to say 'who Christ really is, for us to-day' has, unlike Karl Barth and Dietrich Bonhoeffer, to begin not with Christology, but with anthropology: 'Anthropology and Christology are related to each other as question and answer or (to use Tillich's phrase) they are correlated'.

Like Paul Tillich, then, Dorothee Sölle begins with man, that is, with the question as to who man is, even if he does not (yet) ask any questions. The question, who man is in all his questions, concerns his identity—the identity which he does not *have*, but which he is looking for, since man is 'the being that is not what it is and that is what it is not'. What is this identity which is ahead of us and which, by looking around, we consequently do not find? Dorothee Sölle's answers are scattered throughout her book. Among her answers, we may note the following. Freedom is the New Testament name for identity. Identity was present in the mythical paradise—and in heaven. The kingdom of God is called the kingdom of identity. We look forward to this kingdom in the experience of our non-identity. Our hoping for this future identity in our non-identity allows us no peace—we are restless or, in the words of Augustine, *inquietum est cor nostrum* . . . . Identity cannot be present like something that a person *has* once and for all time—it 'happens' (*sich ereignen*). Identity only happens in relation to another or to others and this other one establishes or these others establish my identity. Man therefore finds his identity together with the other or with others, or he does not find it. It is in being for others that man's search for his own identity comes to rest. Identity is being dependent on the other or on others and this reliance on the other or on others is, in the last resort, a fundamental anthropological structure.

If we replace the word identity in these notes by the word freedom, and the word non-identity by estrangement or alienation, then the connection with Hegel and Marx becomes clear. This does not mean that Dorothee Sölle has taken her anthropology from Hegel—it is not necessary to know much about Hegel to realize that this anthropology is very different from the idealist anthropology—or that hers is a Marxist anthropology. It does mean, however, that she has given elements of nineteenth-century thought the rightful place that has so far been denied to them, certainly by theologians. Where, for example, can we find, in theological anthropology, any acknowledgement of the fact that man's identity also has to do with Marx's 'totality of social relationships'?

After anthropology comes Christology, after the question, answer. Christ is 'the message to the world concerning the real Life'. The New Being of Tillich, or identity, has appeared in him. If we ask, then, what this identity which lies ahead of us consists of, then the answer is—look at him. He is the negation of all the inhuman and 'godless' relationships in which we live. Expressing this idea in brief formulas, we could say that he is our future, that he is precisely where we are not yet, but where we hope to be eventually, that he precedes us on the way to the future (our future), on the way to the kingdom. He is therefore provisionally (this is what distinguishes the representative from the permanent replacer) the precursor who waits for us and looks back at us. Dorothee Sölle uses an excellent German word for this—*Rücksicht,* both in its more usual modern meaning of 'consideration' or 'regard' and in its basic sense of 'looking back'. Christ is not one who permanently and 'inconsiderately', 'without looking back' (*rücksichtslos*), occupies our place and deprives us of our future. He waits for the day when we shall eventually take up our own place and at last find our identity. 'God is not content with our representative. The latter intercedes for us, speaks for us, but we must learn to speak ourselves. He believes for us, but we must learn to believe ourselves. He hopes where we have no hope, but that is not the end of history.' The end of history is that we are led to our place— as God's fellow-workers (1 *Cor.* 3:9), as heirs of his world (*Gal.* 3:29), as men who are called to the freedom of the children of God (*Rom.* 8:21) and as men who live, together with others in the 'totality of social relationships' of Marx, human identity. It is in this way that Christ is our representative, and not as the triumphant Christ at the right hand of the Father, not as the eternal King or as the strong Hero, but as the Servant, suffering with and for men as far as the ultimate consequences of non-identity.

And what about God? God is dead. Christ, however, is not one who replaces the dead God, but one who represents the living God! If we bear in mind how much Dorothee Sölle owes to Hegel, we can perhaps interpret her theo-logy dialectically and say that the death of God is a moment in God's way towards himself and towards his own identity. This amounts to saying that not only man but also God himself is still on the way towards his identity! There are certainly indications in *Stellvertretung* which show that it must be put in this way. God has not yet, like man, 'come to himself'. His identity too lies ahead of him. And once again, Christ is the precursor—not of men now, but of God. Christ is the one who 'acts' God in a world without God, provisionally, that is, until God has found his identity, and God is present in this play. We cannot say who God is and even less can we say who he will be. We can only point to him who acts God and continues to do this as far as death on the cross. *Ecce homo—ecce Deus*! 'That Christ has identified himself with God—this is the only basis that a faith in God can have in our times.'

Finally, Dorothee Sölle's ethics, which we can deal with very briefly. Men are called, provisionally and with all their imperfections and shortcomings, to act together with Christ in the play that he is acting. This could be called the imitation of Christ, but it is better expressed as suffering together with God's suffering in a world without God—Bonhoeffer's theme. This implies being responsible for others as unconditionally as Christ is responsible for us so that they can find their identity, and being there for others and, in being there for others and in no other way, being there for God. In history, after all, on the way to the future, what is involved is both man's identity and that of God. This is probably what the last cryptic sentences of *Stellvertretung* mean—'When the time had been fulfilled, God had done something for us for long enough. He risked himself, made himself dependent on us and identified himself with those who had not found their own identity. Now the time has come for us to do something for God.'

The Beginning of a Map

God

BIBLIOGRAPHY

PAUL Tillich's teaching on God will be found in his *Systematic Theology*, and especially in Part II: *Being and God* (*Systematic Theology I*, pp. 181-321). In this part of his great work, Tillich shows how the *question* of God arises from man's being, defined as finite freedom, and how the Reality of God is the answer to this question. Tillich has written about the dogma of the Trinity at the end of Part IV, after the theology, the Christology and the doctrine about the holy Spirit (see *Systematic Theology III*, pp. 301-14). The indices of the three volumes of the *Systematic Theology* should also be consulted under the headings God, Atheism, Theism etc. Tillich's note on the God beyond God, the nameless and imageless God beyond the God of theism, will be found at the end of his little book, *The Courage to Be*.

In Rudolf Bultmann, one of the essential themes of the kerygma is the act of God in the 'event of Christ', by which men are liberated from the treadmill of care and anxiety. This act of God, however, is not the same as the 'acts of God' of traditional theology. Bultmann rules out any divine intervention in the closed order of nature and history and admits only the miracle of the Word. Many people have questioned whether it is not inconsistent to speak of an act of God in the context of demythologization. Bultmann discusses this question in his essay 'Zum Problem der Entmythologisierung' in *Kerygma und Mythos II* and in the last chapter of his book *Jesus Christ and Mythology* (pp. 69-101). His essay

11

'Zur Frage des Wunders' in *Glauben und Verstehen I*, pp. 214-28, is also of interest in this connection.

When he was writing his letters and making notes in prison —notes which he himself called clumsy and awkward and which he certainly did not regard as in any sense definitive— Bonhoeffer did not for a moment think of the possibility of their being published. What Bonhoeffer has to say in his *Letters and Papers* about God is consequently not set out systematically, but will be found scattered at random throughout the book. Side by side with the contrasting themes of 'religion' and faith in Bonhoeffer's writing, there is also contrast between the helping, paternal God of religion and the God who suffers in the world and is therefore transcendent in the midst of the world. The most important notes on this theme will be found in the letters dated 30 April 1944 (especially pp. 153-5), 8 June 1944, 16 July 1944 (the letter containing the mysterious passage in which the words 'the God who is with us is the God who forsakes us'[1] occur) and 18 July 1944, in the poem 'Christians and Pagans' that follows this letter and in the 'Outline for a Book' that follows the letter of the 3 August 1944.

Robinson's doctrine of God, for which he is greatly indebted to Tillich, will be found at the beginning of *Honest to God*, namely in Chapters 2 and 3. Robinson is violently opposed to theism and calls God the ground of being or the ground of the meaning which is found in life and which is love. He develops his teaching in the discussion with Alasdair MacIntyre printed in *The Honest to God Debate*, pp. 215-31, in his notes on God and on the dogma of the Trinity in the same book, pp. 249-66, and in his speech 'Can a Truly Contemporary Person not be an Atheist?' in *The New Reformation?*, pp. 106-22. In this speech, Robinson accounts for the main reasons for Christian atheism to-day. In *Exploration into God*, which he wrote later, he finds a connection with Martin Buber's ideas about the 'eclipse of God'.

Paul van Buren, Carl Michalson, Gibson Winter and

[1] D. Bonhoeffer, *Letters and Papers from Prison*, 196.

Harvey E. Cox do not treat the doctrine of God systematically. The index to van Buren's *The Secular Meaning of the
Gospel* makes it possible to find his references to God quickly
and what he has to say on this subject is extremely simple—
we have, in bidding farewell to the traditional Christian
doctrine of God, to be silent about God. It is not God himself
who is dead, but the word 'God' that is dead! The books by
the other authors that I have mentioned are without indices.

I have hardly referred at all to Martin Buber in this book
because his thought does not come within the category of
Christian theology. Nonetheless, I should like to mention in
this context his *Eclipse of God. Studies in the Relation between
Religion and Philosophy*, which was published in New York in
1952. In this book, Buber considers in detail the thought of
Martin Heidegger and Jean-Paul Sartre and C. G. Jung's
psychological interpretation of religion. The darkness or
obscuring of God is, in Buber's opinion, connected with the
fact that the I-thou relationship is disappearing—or has
already disappeared. The condition for a new theophany is
that we should learn again really to encounter our fellow-
man.

Helmut Gollwitzer has attacked Christian atheism and
written a vindication of the case (and the need!) for theism
in *The Existence of God as Confessed by Faith*, published by the
Westminster Press of Philadelphia in 1965. Gollwitzer took
up the cudgels in this book for 'biblical faith' against Paul
Tillich, Rudolf Bultmann and Herbert Braun, one of
Bultmann's disciples, but, because the book was originally
published in Germany in 1963, the author was unable to take
into account the most recent developments in England and
the U.S.A. and also in Germany.

In the past, systematic teaching about God was built up
in the following way. There was a knowledge of God to which
man could come by rationally reflecting about reality. Not
only the proofs of the existence of God which Thomas
Aquinas, making use of ancient philosophy and especially
that of Aristotle, included in his *Summa Theologiae*, but also

concepts of God as the Creator, of God's Omnipotence, of his Providence and so on formed part of this 'natural theology'. Beside and above this natural theology, there was also a knowledge of God which came from his word or revelation. There was thus a harmony of nature and grace. This twofold knowledge of God was raised to the status of dogma by the First Vatican Council in the dogmatic constitution *Dei Filius* and the Council pronounced its anathema on atheists, agnostics and many others who believed that the possibility of proofs of the existence of God and so on had to be denied.

This synthesis of nature and grace was broken by Luther, who asserted that God is only known to man from his Word. Luther was not thinking in the first place of the Bible here, but of God's contingent historical revelation, of the Word— the Logos—of John 1:14. But the infrastructure of natural theology returned in Melanchthon's teaching, even though the relationship between nature and grace here was less harmonious than in Roman Catholic theology. In its further development, orthodox Protestant teaching was very little different from that of medieval scholasticism. In the nineteenth century, this predominantly medieval and Aristotelian way of thinking in Protestant theology was superseded by a modern 'philosophy of religion', for example, that of idealism. This happened in the case of Schleiermacher.

The great revolution in theology, started by Karl Barth and his *Epistle to the Romans*, was directed among other things against natural theology, the nineteenth-century type of 'philosophy of religion' and the analogy of being between the Infinite and the finite, which is the condition for natural theology and which Barth regarded as an invention of the Antichrist. We know God only (where and whenever he makes himself known) from his revelation which, so to speak, descends into our lives perpendicularly from above and is at right angles to our entire experience and to all human religiosity and is the κρίσις of everything that we are and do and think. Faith does not live on the eternal truths, but on what Lessing called the 'chance truth of history'. A new biblical theology is here coupled with the experience of the 'historicity' of human existence and a return to the reformers. No religious metaphysics, no 'philosophy of religion', but a return to matter-of-fact objectivity—'to the matters themselves', the slogan of the phenomenologists.

The new theology is solidly behind Karl Barth in its opposition to natural theology. Bonhoeffer, for example, said in his 'Outline for a Book', the book that he was planning to write: 'Who is God? Not in the first place an abstract belief in God, in his omnipotence etc. That is not a genuine experience of God, but a partial extension of the world. Encounter with Jesus Christ. The experience that a transformation of all human life is given . . .'[1] That Bonhoeffer had accepted as much of Karl Barth's teaching in the *Church Dogmatics* here as he did in his unmasking of religion emerges quite clearly from these short sentences. Tillich, on the other hand, strictly followed out his correlation of philosophy and theology, insisting that revelation does not descend into our lives perpendicularly from above, but provides the answer to our questions, and used such philosophical formulas as 'God is Being itself' (*ipsum esse*). But even he would have nothing to do with natural theology. We only know who God is from his revelation and from no other source. Man can say nothing about God from himself— he can only ask about God. No man can guarantee that God will answer—that he is there as the Answer!

This is also the case in the further development of the new theology. It is so even when these new theologians are increasingly silent about God, in accordance with their avowed anti-metaphysical tendency. Christian faith is always orientation in the world, an orientation that is found in the story of the Old and New Testaments. And that story deals with historical events. The things which determine the 'discernment' of faith happened, for example, 'in the days of Caesar Augustus', in other words, in history. 'Men of Galilee, why do you stand looking into heaven?' (*Acts* 1:11). The

[1]*Op. cit.*, 209.

heaven of the eternal truths—God is, he is almighty, he is the creator of the world and so on—is empty. We live here on earth, in history. Orientation in history is the theme of the new theology.

This is not the only instance where the new theologians firmly reject the older theological tradition. They also reject what was known until recently as the 'Christian image of God'. The twentieth century could be described as the great iconoclastic age, comparable to the breaking of images in the Old and New Testaments of the gods of the *gôîm*, the other nations—the images of wood, stone and terra cotta—and to the Old Testament smashing of the images of Yahweh which were set up to make him, the nameless God, visible to men.

The new theology is also opposed to theism, to the God who, as the eternal Person dwelling in heaven, rules the earth in the manner described on the tenth Sunday of the Heidelberg catechism, that is, in such a way that 'riches and poverty and all things come to us not by chance, but from his paternal hand': God's hand, in other words, the omnipotence of his love, makes everything what it is and God goes his own way without accounting for his unfathomable counsel. This is, expressed very briefly, the theist idea of God, which Bultmann called mythological and Robinson and Tillich call supranatural. It is unanimously rejected by all the new theologians.

Various themes are combined in the struggle against theism. I list a few of these below:

1. The scandal caused by everything that has been done in history in the name of 'God'. It is God's will! This was said said by the Inquisition. It was said at the time of the religious wars of the seventeenth century and during the period of misery and squalor among the European proletariat of the nineteenth century. It has been said on many different occasions and anyone who is familiar with the social history of the nineteenth century can easily imagine the indignation that Karl Marx, that prophet and Prometheus of the times, must have felt whenever he listened to all the 'talk about God' that

went on in those days and the scorn that lay behind his description of religion as 'false consciousness'. So much for the nineteenth century. What about our own? What does God stand for in the twentieth century? Of what social and political realities is he the symbol now? If the word 'God' is really dead, as Paul van Buren has placed on record, then we have also to admit that no attempt has been spared to kill it.

2. The scandal caused by the fact that everything that happens must be attributed to God or to his 'paternal hand' or, if it is not his will, then at least he permits it to happen. The theist idea of God has not only been smashed to pieces by the countless times that the third commandment (*Exod.* 20:7) has been broken, but also, and even more, by the question of theodicy. How can the problem of grief in the world be reconciled with the rule of an omnipotent and loving God? It was possible for Leibniz to say that, although we do not live in a perfect world, we do live in the best of all possible worlds, that is, of all conceivable worlds. But this no longer works and it will never work again. Too much has happened—and nothing happened. 'The face of God after Auschwitz!' In his lecture on atheism, John A. T. Robinson records the words of a girl who had written faith off—'Religion is disgusting'. One is reminded of Dostoievski's Ivan Karamazov.

3. The fact that we have become estranged from the older world-view in which God, as it were, had the run of the house and provided for us when we had nothing left. But, whether we like it or not, our present idea of the world is determined by what could be called the law of continuity. We no longer count on God's intervening and we are no longer able to count on it. We no longer believe in miracles—all that we know still (if we know it at all!) is the miracle of the Word that makes everything new. Who are the 'we' of these sentences? I thought at first that I would be bound to say everybody in the twentieth century, all of us who do not know the way back to the ancient image of the world. But I am now convinced that the first and second themes in the struggle

against theism are more important than this theme, although more has been written about this one.

4. If we are to describe the situation fully, something must be said about the part played by contemporary philosophy in the struggle against theism as well as about the part played by a new biblical theology of the type of Martin Buber's in which the eternal Thou, without any name or any image, leads his people on their way towards the future. We do not know who he is, but 'I shall be as who I shall be' (*Exod.* 3:14 in Buber's translation). I can do no more than draw attention to this theme here.

SPEAKING OR SILENCE

WHAT follows this departure from theism? I will mention a few of the possibilities that have been mapped out in the new theology.

1. It is possible to say that we still have to go on using the word God, however torn, battered and worn out it is. Martin Buber does, for example. It is certainly possible to continue to use it, but it is only a credible word so long as it is used on the margin of silence and covered and substantiated by an act which makes peace and brings about justice.

2. It is possible, from biblical and traditional data, to construct a new doctrine of God by looking for a way—as narrow as a tight-rope walker's rope!—between theism and atheist naturalism. Paul Tillich followed this path in his *Systematic Theology*, calling God Being itself (*ipsum esse*), the ground and the power of Being which includes itself and its world and the Reality which is inconceivable to thought and is in and through itself. We cannot really say any more than this—the rest is silence. But silence is impossible because Being is being said. We speak—symbolically. This means we speak in terms which we derive from our world and from our own reality in the to and from of *sic et non*. So we say, God is like this—he is the Creator, the Shepherd, 'our Father in heaven'. And yet, God is not like this. He is different. He is

the absolutely Different one. There is no name that names him and no word that expresses him. He is the abyss, silence, Nothing. In saying and not saying, our thought is a moth fluttering around the black light. Everything finds its place in the gossamer-thin fabric of the *Systematic Theology*—the great symbols of religion and the profound definitions of mystical theology and God is all of this and he is not any of it. But, we ask, does it refer to anything? Tillich's answer is that it refers to the Reality which, with its *parousia*, its being with us, gives us, in our finite freedom, the courage to be. We express this reality when we say—God.

3. It is also possible to construct a theology entirely on the basis of Jesus, the Servant of Yahweh, of whom the Church says that God has spoken in him to us men. This is the path followed by Dietrich Bonhoeffer. The God of religion—the omnipotent, paternal, helping God, to whom insignificant man entrusts himself with all his cares—is no longer there. He has disappeared along with religion. We can no longer be religious. We are simply not allowed to be. But, in reading the story of the New Testament, the story of the man who lived his life entirely for the people he encountered on his way, we encounter God. Jesus's ' "being there for others" is the experience of transcendence,'[1] Bonhoeffer said in his 'Outline for a Book'. It is there that not only life lives from God, but also all thought about God must begin. Anything that we may be able to say about the God of faith is an explication of this 'datum'. Jesus is the one who was crucified— and the God of faith is the God who suffers in the world, the crucified, despised, poor, dead God without power.

For Christians and pagans alike he hangs dead and it is only in this way, with this presage, that anything can be said about God's omnipotence, his omniscience and his omnipresence and about the power of God and his wisdom (see 1 *Cor.* 1:24-5). But what this is Bonhoeffer was not able to say. We must simply guess and take Bonhoeffer's advice to heart, as given in the letter of 21 August 1944: 'The God of Jesus Christ has nothing

[1] *Op. cit.,* 209.

to do with what God, as we imagine him, could do and ought to do . . . We must persevere in quiet meditation on the life, sayings, deeds, sufferings, and death of Jesus.'[1]

We have only to take one more step along the path of this thought, that God is at one with the crucified Jesus and underwent himself the death of the cross, and we reach the death of God. Bonhoeffer himself did not, however, take this step. Particularly in his last letters and in the poem 'Powers of Good' which he wrote at the very end of 1944, Bonhoeffer referred to the caring Presence of 'the God who forsakes us.'[2] 'God does not give us everything we want, but he does fulfil all his promises, i.e. he remains the Lord of the earth, he preserves his Church, constantly renewing our faith and not laying on us more than we can bear, . . . hearing our prayers, and leading us along the best and straightest paths to himself.'[3] And

> While all the powers of good aid and attend us,
> Boldly we'll face the future, come what may.
> At even and at morn God will befriend us,
> And oh, most surely on each New Year's Day!

4. The step towards the death of God was, however, taken later, first in America and then in Germany. Now we must take care to distinguish who or what is dead—the word God, our theist idea of God or God himself. In the case of Paul van Buren and Harvey E. Cox, it is the first and the second that are dead. This has to do with the non-metaphysical, empirical attitude of these two theologians. They cannot say that God himself is dead, because, assuming that he is, how can we know it? But the word G-o-d, which has caused so much confusion and around which so many out-of-date ideas have crystallized, must be avoided and we must be silent about G-o-d. T. R. Miles still takes the possibility into

[1] *Op. cit.*, 213.
[2] *Op. cit.*, 196.
[3] *Op. cit.*, 213.

account that this silence may occasionally be broken or 'qualified' by likenesses which evoke the word God, such as the gospel accounts. Harvey E. Cox, however, does not admit this possibility: 'It may well be that our English word *God* will have to die, corroborating in some measure Nietzsche's apocalyptic judgment that "God is dead." '[1] The liberating Presence has not, however, disappeared with the word G-o-d. X will be there, even in the future without God, and he will have a new name, just as he was so often given a new name in the Old Testament, because

> Every series, every connection,
> whatever language it is taken from,
> is suitable, so long as the voltage is right.
>
> G. Achterberg.

But these new words have not yet been found and the new language—'It will be a new language' (Bonhoeffer)—or the old language renewed are not there yet. We have to wait for God's time, for the Time. A period has come to a close and is closed for good. That is expressed in the formula 'God is dead'. The end of a period—but the end of the theist period is not the end of Christian faith. The mood of the theology that begins with the death of God—not ends, but begins!— is one of expectation and trust. In God? In the one without any name, without any image, without form, unknown and hidden, the one who goes with us on the way to Emmaus. On the way, Scripture is interpreted. And in Emmaus itself, bread is broken. 'I shall be as who I shall be.'

[1] H. E. Cox, *The Secular City*, London 1965, 265.

Revelation

BIBLIOGRAPHY

PAUL Tillich has written in some detail about revelation in his *Systematic Theology* (see especially Part I: *Reason and Revelation, Systematic Theology I*, pp. 79-180). Tillich shows here how reason is driven by its own inner contradictions to the quest for revelation and how the answer is given in revelation. Further indications will be found in the indices under Revelation, Revelatory experiences, etc. Tillich's arguments about the Spiritual Presence in his *Systematic Theology III* are also of importance in this connection. A good summary of his conception of revelation will be found in Alexander J. McKelway's *The Systematic Theology of Paul Tillich*, pp. 71-102.

For Rudolf Bultmann, revelation is more or less synonymous with what he called the act of God or the event of Christ. I would therefore refer the reader back to the bibliography at the beginning of the previous chapter. In addition, there are two relevant articles in *Glauben und Verstehen*—'Der Begriff des Wortes Gottes im Neuen Testament' (*Glauben und Verstehen I*, pp. 268-93) and 'Die Frage der natürlichen Offenbarung' (*Glauben und Verstehen III*, pp. 1-34). The second was written in 1941, a long time before Bultmann became explicitly concerned with his theme of demythologization, but it does throw considerable light on his idea of revelation. Walter Schmithals gives a good summary of Bultmann's view of revelation in his *Theologie Rudolf Bultmanns*, pp. 151-75.

Bonhoeffer has very little to say about revelation in his *Letters and Papers*, but it seems to me that his concept of revelation is very close to that of Karl Barth, although he does once or twice accuse Barth of positivism on revelation (in the letters dated 30 April 1944 and 5 May 1944) and says that Barth's positivist doctrine here is in the last analysis a theology of restoration. In any case, for Bonhoeffer too, Christ is the revelation of God.

Very little systematic thought about the concept of revelation can be found in John A. T. Robinson's books. In *Honest to God* p. 106 ff., however, he challenges Julian Huxley's 'Religion without Revelation' and says that Christ is the disclosure of the definitive truth in relation to man, the whole of nature and the whole of reality, but, as in the case of Bonhoeffer, there is a great deal that is not made clear.

For Paul van Buren, revelation is the event which, received in faith, gives man a new 'blik' of reality. In his description of this event, van Buren uses such words as 'discernment' and 'disclosure', which he has taken from Ian T. Ramsey. The most important passages in *The Secular Meaning of the Gospel* will be found in the index under Revelation.

In the theology of the death of God, there is no reference to revelation, probably because the word is too reminiscent of the 'language game' of traditional theology. There is, however, a 'situation' of revelation in this theology insofar as life and thought in the situation of the death of God remain orientated towards the story of the Bible.

The logical consequence of the repudiation of natural theology (see p. 148 ff.) has been the rejection of 'natural revelation'. The new theologians regard revelation as a historical event. This means that revelation is an existential event which changes the lives of men (the German theologians use the word *geschichtlich* in this context) and that this existential event is connected with the history of Jesus of Nazareth as told in the Bible. But there is more to it than simply a rejection of 'natural revelation'. To understand this, we must go back in history.

If we limit ourselves to what used to be called, in the past, 'supernatural revelation', we may say that this revelation was thought of above all as the disclosure of truths which man, by his reason, could not find himself—the disclosure, for example, of 'the mysteries hidden in God', as the First Vatican Council said in its dogmatic constitution *Dei Filius*. God directed himself in his revelation to man's intellect and, it should be added, to his will. It was, after all, not simply a question of our knowing these mysteries, but also of our following the way of salvation. This idea could be expressed in an extreme form by saying that God did not reveal himself, but revealed truths about himself, about man, about the world, about the past and the future and about the way of salvation. These truths were the *credenda*, what had to be believed, and these *credenda* were expressed by the Church in her dogmas.

The Roman Catholic Church tells us that these truths have been given to us 'in written books and in unwritten traditions' as the Tridentine formula expressed it, in other words, in Scripture and tradition and in the pronouncements of the teaching office of the Church. The Churches of the Reformation and orthodox Protestantism, on the other hand, have limited themselves to *sola Scriptura*—Scripture alone. Here and there, however, revelation was conceived as the communication of truths which, although not contrary to reason, nonetheless transcended reason and which were systematized in the teaching of the Church. A great deal of value was naturally attached to the reliability of this information and so the Church came to be infallible in Roman Catholicism, and Scripture to be infallible in Protestantism. The infallibility of Scripture led, in Protestant theology, to the absurd doctrine of the literal inspiration of the Bible. All the words, all the letters and all the punctuation marks in Scripture had been directly inspired by the holy Spirit himself. Hollaz, a Lutheran theologian of the seventeenth century, vindicated this doctrine in a choice syllogism:

Quicquid deus revelavit infallibiliter verum est.
Quicquid sacra scriptura docet, illud deus revelavit.
Ergo:
Quicquid sacra scriptura docet infallibiliter verum
est.

(Everything that God has revealed is infallibly true. Everything that Holy Scripture teaches has been revealed by God.
Therefore everything that Holy Scripture teaches is infallibly true.)

This 'infallible truth' thus included the story of the six
days of creation, that of the serpent which spoke to Eve and
that of the sun which stood still at Joshua's command. This
fundamentalism was the logical and fatal consequence of the
conviction that revelation was information which had at all
costs to be reliable. And the consequence of this fundamentalism was the conflict between 'faith' and science in which
truth fought against truth and both refused to yield an inch.

Faith (although I shall be coming back to this later) in this
situation was obedient submission to God's authority and
consequently, for the Protestant believer, to Scripture and,
for the Catholic believer, to the Church. For thousands, this
is still Christian faith—the state of having not yet come of
age (Bonhoeffer), immaturity for which man has only
himself to blame (Kant), consistent heteronomy and the
positivism of revelation.

Bonhoeffer was probably thinking of all this past history
when he described Karl Barth's theology (whether rightly or
wrongly does not concern us here) as a positivist doctrine of
revelation. That at least is what is indicated in the letter of
5 May 1944, in which Bonhoeffer wrote that Barth had made
faith, God's 'gift for us', into a law (this is what you must
believe—'like it or lump it'),[1] meaning that, on closer
examination, what Barth had done was to continue the old
theology in a new orthodoxy. This too is what Paul Tillich
noticed about the development of Barth's theology—that it

[1] D. Bonhoeffer, *Letters and Papers from Prison*, 157.

grew from the kerygmatic theology of the *Epistle to the Romans* towards the new orthodoxy of the *Church Dogmatics*.

All the same, it cannot be denied that the great renewal in Protestant theology began with Karl Barth and this is not disputed by Tillich or Bultmann or Bonhoeffer. In broad outline, this is what Barth said on the subject of revelation: we know God *only* from his Word, but that Word does not coincide with the Bible. God's Word is *only* the revelation, in other words, Jesus Christ, who is in any case called the Word (*logos*) in John 1. It is here only, and nowhere else, that an 'equals' is possible without any reservation and without their being any possibility of disputing it. We do know of God's Word only through the Bible and preaching. It does not come to us from nature or from history and we do not hear it in the voice of conscience or in mystical contemplation. We do have to rely completely on the Bible and preaching for the Word of God, and the 'biblical concentration' is indeed the direct consequence of the 'Christological concentration'. But the Bible *is* not the Word of God. It can become the Word of God if the Word itself (Christ) addresses us in the Bible—if, to use Bultmann's term, the Bible become kerygma. But men cannot possibly make that happen—if it does, it is not because of men. We can only place on record that it does happen, wherever and whenever God wills it and not otherwise. In itself, then, the Bible is man's testimony of God's Word. It is not the Word itself. That is why Barth was able to accept without difficulty the case made out by historical and critical biblical scholarship—which was quite different from elaborating the findings of this historical and critical research—and to oppose what he called the 'fatal doctrine of inspiration'. If matters stand thus, the Bible, that human testimony of God's Word, can no longer be read as a book containing all kinds of information. Hollaz could say *Quicquid deus revelavit* ..., 'Everything that God has revealed ...', but Barth could not. God has not revealed all kinds of things. God reveals himself, wherever and whenever he wills it, and he reveals himself as God with us, the God of the Covenant, the God of

(salvation) history and the Father of Jesus Christ. That is the
'matter of Scripture'. Once again, then, we come 'to the
matters themselves'. We cannot deny that there is a great
gulf between the theology of Karl Barth and that of the
seventeenth century. And yet ... Did Bonhoeffer really make
a mistake in calling Barth's theology positivism of revelation?
The serpent did speak and the grave is empty. Everything
comes back—the Trinity, the Virgin Mary and so on. Faith
in the form of a law—this is what you must believe!

Bultmann went farther along the path taken by Barth. The
Bible is not itself the Word of God, but the human testimony
of that Word. It can become the Word of God, kerygma, and
that happens whenever it discloses to men here and now that
they have come to belong to an older world and whenever
these men allow themselves to be summoned and called away
from this older world to a life of faith, love and simplicity.
There is no question any longer in Bultmann's theology of
information (about God, man, the world and so on) in the
Bible. In his essay 'Der Begriff der Offenbarung im Neuen
Testament' in the collection *Glauben und Versgehen III,* he
wrote: 'What is revealed, then? Nothing, insofar as the quest
for revelation demands a doctrine which man would not have
come upon himself or mysteries which—once they have been
disclosed—would be known once and for all time. Everything, insofar as man's eyes are opened to his own situation'.
The first part of the answer to the question 'what is revealed?'
must be retained as consistently as the second—nothing and
everything. The man who believes, who has really heard the
kerygma, *knows* no more about God, man, the world or the
future, but he has become a different man—himself. *Inquietum
est cor nostrum* ... 'Our hearts are restless ...'—Bultmann
frequently quotes these words of Augustine. But now our
hearts are no longer restless.

> Elle est retrouvée!
> Quoi?—L'éternité.

Arthur Rimbaud.

12

'That is why, at the end of his last discourse in the gospel of John, Jesus could say, as the fulfilment of revelation, that there would be nothing more to ask (*John* 16:23 f.) . . . Man has become transparent to himself—he has become "light". That Jesus is the light which enlightens men does not mean that he gives men an ability to know (or that he increases that ability), so that the things of the world are illuminated, but that he makes them light.'

That is the 'event of Christ', the event of salvation, the act of God or whatever else we care to call it. It is not information, but the 'communication of existence', to use Kierkegaard's phrase, the thinker from whom Bultmann took so much. The event of Christ is thus enacted now—it always takes place in the present where a man is crucified to his older world, that treadmill, and rises to a new life. Now, the only question that remains is what conceivable connection is there between the fact that a Jewish rabbi was crucified somewhere in the region of Jerusalem during the reign of the Emperor Tiberius (we may assume that this crucifixion really took place) and the event of Christ that changes my life (or, if we think in terms of the eschatological community, our lives)? What conceivable link is there, in other words, between the faith of the disciples that the crucified Christ rose from his grave (we cannot establish historically any more than simply that *faith*) and the fact that my life has become light? We can certainly say that the eschatological community of men whose lives are changed and who have become light came about at that time and that there is a historical connection. But is there also a theological, material connection between the saving event (in the present!) and these happenings which may or may not have been historical? Or must we say that the account of Christ's crucifixion and resurrection is the mythological expression of that transition from darkness into light, of that becoming light of the existence that is faith and life itself? If so, we should be bound, by demythologization and *Existenzialinterpretation*, to make the significance of this account clear as well—it would be

more important to do so here than anywhere else in the
gospel, and we could hardly do so in any other way than by
transposing it from the past into the present. But then we
are confronted by the question as to why the account began
there, in the region of Jerusalem, and at that time, during the
reign of the Emperor Tiberius, and not somewhere else and
at a different time. If we are to answer this question, Bultmann says, we must go back to the time before the crucifixion
and encounter the Lord there, since he had already risen to
the eschatological existence in faith, love, simplicity and
freedom before he was crucified. If my interpretation of
Bultmann's view of the 'event of Christ' is correct, then it is
not difficult to see why 'research into the life of Jesus' was
recommenced in Bultmann's school.

It is also clear that Paul van Buren is close to Bultmann
here. In van Buren's view, the 'discernment' of the disciples,
their certainty that 'this is it', resulted from Jesus's freedom.
This certainty, the certainty that 'this is it', is revelation.
There is no question, in the case of van Buren, of revelation
being information about God, man, the world or the future,
although there is—and here van Buren differs from Bultmann
—a clear connection with the historical Jesus. It was Jesus's
freedom that was catching and renewed others. It is, however,
possible that this connection is also present in the case of
Bultmann, but here his texts are shrouded in a thick mist—
a mist which even Walter Schmithals has not been able to
dispel.

There is another thing which emerges very clearly from
the writings of both Bultmann and van Buren. This is that
there can be no question in their theology of that conflict
between faith and science in which both orthodox Protestantism and traditional Roman Catholicism have become
entangled. The independence of the sciences is not only not
disputed, it is also emphatically recognized. There is scope
for all the theories and hypotheses that scientists wish to put
forward. What reason could faith possibly have for opposing,
for example, the theory of evolution? A faith which explains

nothing and which therefore does not provide explanations which are different from those of science (if science really does explain anything!), a faith that is also a 'blik' of the history by which life is changed—this faith has nothing to 'defend'. It is there, not as a system of pronouncements about God, man, the world and the future or as a view of the world, but as a lived reality and this puts an end to the age-old conflict between faith and science. Even reason has its function in faith, as Carl Michalson points out, not as obedient submission to Scripture or to the Church, but in that once the believer has seen the light, it is his task to use all his power of thought (and imagination) to see what the history that is handed down to us in the gospels means in his situation. That is the reason why Carl Michalson gave his book the manifesto-like title of *The Rationality of Faith*.

There is also no contradiction between faith and science in Paul Tillich. This is so simply because God does not give any answers to the questions that men ask, but *is* himself the answer and because this answer refers only to the existential questions—anxiety, estrangement, 'the life we have lost in living' (T. S. Eliot)—and not to all kinds of other questions which a man may ask. 'Revelation . . . cannot be introduced into the context of ordinary knowledge as an addition',[1] but life is discovered and estrangement is ended.

Tillich has given a splendid description of revelation in the first part of his *Systematic Theology*. Revelation is seen as miracle. This miracle is not a disruption or a cancelling out of the order of nature or history in accordance with the older definition of miracle, but reality's becoming transparent, so that it becomes real in a way that is quite different from its previous reality. Tillich notes that the New Testament often used the word 'sign' in this context and prefers himself to speak of a 'sign-event'. Wherever something acquires the character of a sign-event which causes astonishment, there is revelation. But nothing is simply in itself, objectively, a sign-event. An occurrence is only a sign-event if it is seen,

[1] P. Tillich, *Systematic Theology I*, London 1964, 143.

noticed and received. In his description of revelation, Tillich speaks not only of the miracle or sign-event, but also of the ecstasy which sees this miracle. Ecstasy here has nothing to do with emotional states or with the confusion of tongues discussed by Paul in 1 Corinthians 14:1-25. It is the astonishment which notices the miracle. With no ecstasy of the spirit, there is no miracle. There are people who 'see but do not perceive . . . hear but do not understand' (*Mark* 4:12). The reality is 'opaque'—there is nothing to see. The people of Nazareth saw the carpenter, the son of Mary, and nothing else (*Mark* 6:3): there is nothing else and one must not imagine that there is. There is no miracle and no ecstasy. Nothing happens. Peter saw something more, something quite different: 'You are the Christ' (*Mark* 8:29). And, although others could say that nothing had happened, the miracle and the ecstasy are there. He is it. What? That cannot be said. It can only be described by powerful symbols such as the Messiah, the Son of God and so on. He is the Reality. He is the truth, the life, the light, the way—the miracle. These are the words that have to be used in a 'revelatory correlation'.

Tillich does not say therefore that Jesus, as the Christ, is the only revelation. There is also authentic revelation in the Old Testament—in, for example, the great vision of Isaiah described in Isaiah 6. There is even a genuine 'revelatory correlation' outside the Bible and in the most primitive forms of religiosity. 'There is no reality, thing, or event which cannot become the bearer of the mystery of being and enter into a revelatory correlation.'[1] Revelation does not descend vertically from above as it does in the teaching of Karl Barth. Tillich gives us a history of revelation. But the *kairos*, the central point of history, is for Christianity, the revelation in Jesus as the Christ. There is, then, in this respect, a 'Christological concentration' in Tillich's doctrine of revelation. The last word has been spoken in Christ. He is the final revelation. 'This claim establishes a Christian Church, and, where this

[1] *Op. cit.*, 131.

claim is absent, Christianity has ceased to exist.'[1] I believe that Tillich is right here, although he was wrong to try to vindicate this claim with rational arguments. It is, after all, a question of either/or. Either a person is in this 'revelatory correlation' of faith, in which case he can only say that Jesus is indeed the Christ, light, truth and so on, or he is outside it, in which case he cannot be convinced by arguments. Faith is not founded on arguments, but on what Ian T. Ramsey and, with him, Paul van Buren have called a 'discernment', and it takes a risk on what it has seen and what can always be doubted again. But this is taking us beyond revelation and on to faith.

[1] Op. cit., 147.

Christ

BIBLIOGRAPHY

HISTORICAL research into the life of Jesus was recommenced
by members of Rudolf Bultmann's school and especially by
Ernst Käsemann, Günther Bornkamm, Gerhard Ebeling and
Ernst Fuchs. The following are the most important documents in this research: Ernst Käsemann, 'Das problem des
historischen Jesus', *Zeitschrift für Theologie und Kirche LI*, 1954,
pp. 125-53; Günther Bornkamm, *Jesus von Nazareth*, Stuttgart 1956, published in the series *Urban Bücher*, No. 19;
Gerhard Ebeling, 'Die Frage nach dem historischen Jesus
und das Problem der Christologie', *Zeitschrift für Theologie
und Kirche, Beiheft I*, 1959, pp. 14-111; various articles by
Ernst Fuchs, including 'Die Frage nach dem historischen
Jesus', *Zeitschrift für Theologie und Kirche LIII*, 1956, pp. 210-29
and 'Glaube und Geschichte im Blick auf die Frage nach dem
historischen Jesus', *Zeitschrift für Theologie und Kirche LIV*,
1957, pp. 117-56. The last two articles were included in a
larger collection edited by Ernst Fuchs and published as a
book by J. C. B. Mohr of Tübingen in 1960, entitled *Zur
Frage nach dem historischen Jesus*. A good introduction to this
new research into the life of Jesus was published in 1959 by
the SCM Press of London: James M. Robinson's *A New
Quest of the Historical Jesus*. H. Zahrnt's *Es begann mit Jesus von
Nazareth*, Kreuz Verlag, Stuttgart 1960, is, however, simpler
and more suitable as a first orientation in the subject.

Paul Tillich's Christology will be found in his *Systematic
Theology* and especially in Part III, *Existence and the Christ*

167

(*Systematic Theology II*, pp. 19-208). There are also important notes on Christology in *Systematic Theology I*, pp. 147-53 (the chapter on Jesus as the final revelation) and in *Systematic Theology III*, pp. 153-9. Tillich's most fundamental christological idea is that it is in Jesus that the New Being has manifested itself in history and that he is the answer to man's estrangement (from himself), which leads to the search for the New Being. Other references to the subject of Christ will be found in the indices of the *Systematic Theology* under Christ, Christology, New Being and so on.

As for Rudolf Bultmann, his most important statement is contained in that part of his essay 'The New Testament and Mythology' in *Kerygma and Myth* (New York, 1961) which deals with the event of Christ and in which an 'existential' interpretation of the crucifixion and the resurrection is given. Bultmann believes that Jesus's crucifixion was a historical event which was interpreted mythologically in the kerygma of the first Christian community, but that the resurrection was not a historical event. Of dogmatic importance is the essay 'Das christologische Bekenntnis des Oekumenischen Rates' in the collection *Glauben und Verstehen II*, Tübingen 1952, pp. 246-61, a critical examination of the formula in which Jesus Christ is spoken of as 'God and Saviour'. Once again, Walter Schmithals provides a good summary of Bultmann's ideas about the crucifixion and resurrection in *Die Theologie Rudolf Bultmanns*, pp. 129-50.

There is, of course, no systematic Christology in Bonhoeffer's *Letters and Papers*. Bonhoeffer emphasizes Christ's suffering and crucifixion (Christ as the suffering servant of Yahweh in *Is.* 53) which, for him, was the ultimate consequence of Christ's being for others.

There is a connection between Bonhoeffer and John A. T. Robinson, who has given a broad outline of his Christology in the fourth chapter of his *Honest to God*, entitled 'The Man for Others', in which he also discusses his attitude towards the christological dogma defined by the Church in 451 at the Council of Chalcedon.

Paul van Buren's book, *The Secular Meaning of the Gospel*, is entirely concerned with Christology, and especially in Part Two. The following sections are particularly important: his analysis of the christological dogma, pp. 23-47, his own Christology of 'call' and 'response', pp. 47-55, the chapter on Jesus of Nazareth, pp. 109-34, in which he makes use of the recent research into the historical Jesus, and his analysis of the language of New Testament and patristic Christology, pp. 145-56 and 159-68. In the new American theology, Carl Michalson's book, *The Rationality of Faith*, is also important, especially the passage dealing with the resurrection, pp. 48-56 and the part in which he describes Jesus's work as the liberation of man to historical responsibility.

Perhaps the most remarkable Christology of recent years, however, is that of Dorothee Sölle, who combines themes from Tillich and Bonhoeffer with the idea of Jesus as the 'representative' and as the true teacher.

The ancient Church made two classical statements about Christ. The first is the *Symbolum Apostolicum*, better known as the Creed or the twelve articles of faith, which was developed from the short confession of faith that was used at baptism in the community of Rome. The second is the christological dogma which was defined in 451 at the Council of Chalcedon for the purpose of ending the controversy about Christology that took place in the first Christian centuries. In one sense, the Council of Nicea was also concerned in the year 325 with Christology, namely, with the relationship of the Son—the *Logos* or the Word—to the Father.

The second part of the *Symbolum Apostolicum*, which was called the *summa* of the *fides catholica et indubitata* in the Heidelberg Catechism, says:

> (I believe)
> in Jesus Christ, his only begotten Son, our Lord,
> who was conceived by the Holy Ghost,
> born of the Virgin Mary;

suffered under Pontius Pilate,
was crucified, dead and buried;
he descended into hell;
the third day he rose again from the dead;
he ascended into heaven,
sitteth at the right hand of God
the Father Almighty;
from thence he shall come to judge
the living and the dead.

The Creed thus gives a summary of the facts in the past, the present and the future, the facts that determine our lives as the 'facts of salvation'.

But the Church did not simply wish to say what Christ did, what he does and what he will do. She also wanted to say who Christ is. This was done in the dogmatic definitions of the first Christian centuries, in which, with the aid of Greek philosophy (it could hardly have been done differently), such words as *physis* (nature), *ousia* (substance) and *hypostasis* (person) were used to define the mystery of Christ. The Council of Nicea thus affirmed that the Son was one in substance with the Father, but was nonetheless distinct from the Father. In the Nicene formula, it was positively stated that Christ was *vere Deus*, truly God, and the Council of Chalcedon added that he was also *vere homo*, truly man. According to the *Symbolum Chalcedonense*, then, there were two 'natures' in Christ, the divine nature and the human nature, and these two natures were one, being joined in the one person (*hypostasis*). For the rest, the *Symbolum Chalcedonense* was an attempt to find the dialectical balance between the unity and the two natures of Christ, without prejudicing either this unity or the necessary distinction between the two natures within this unity. Christ was thus truly God and truly man, and the Christmas story of the Heidelberg Catechism (Sunday XIV) referred to the event in which 'the eternal Son of God, who is and remains truly and eternally God, assumed true human nature'. A good short account of the way to Chalcedon is given by Paul van Buren in *The Secular Meaning of the Gospel*, pp. 23-33.

The Christology that I have briefly outlined above was the common property both of Roman Catholicism and of the various branches of reformed Christianity. The 'facts of salvation' stated in the Apostles' Creed were without exception conceived realistically. The Mother of God was really a virgin and always remained a virgin. Jesus really descended into the hell below the earth after his death and he rose again from the dead and his grave was empty. There was, in the theology of the Reformation, a cautious 'demythologization' of the descent into hell, which is hardly to be found in the New Testament, but for the rest the realistic conception of the facts of salvation stood firm. Of course it did, because it was in the (fundamentally conceived) Bible, which was the Word of God.

In the eighteenth century, during which the structure of classical dogmatism was undermined by, among other things, historical and critical study of the Bible, the historical Jesus was, however, set against the Christ of dogmatism. This movement began with Reimarus, whose essays on the gospels, the most important of which was 'Vom Zwecke Jesu und seiner Jünger', were published by Lessing as *Fragmente eines Ungenannten*. This book was followed in the eighteenth and nineteenth centuries by a long series of books on the life of Jesus. The aim of these authors was to discover the historical reality of Jesus of Nazareth behind the gospel accounts and dogmatic Christology. They were sustained in their search by the conviction that it was certainly possible to apply the historical and critical method to the gospels (the only 'sources' at their disposal) and thus to get on the track of this historical reality. The discouraging result, however, was that idealism found an idealist Jesus, romanticism found a romantic Jesus and liberal theology found a liberal Jesus. Their discovery was like that of Novalis's young man, who raised the veil of the goddess Isis.

And what did he see? He saw, wonder of wonders,
himself!

At the end of this long series of books there is Albert
Schweitzer's great work, *Die Geschichte der Leben-Jesu-
Forschung,* and then there is silence. It is not possible, with
the facts that we possess, to trace the historical reality.

This is closely related to the fact that the gospels are not
chronicles providing a meticulous record of what happened.
They are kerygma, preaching, proclamation, the testimony
of the first Christian community and of its faith in the Lord.
This means that the representation of the facts—but what
are facts?—and the interpretation of these facts are indissolubly linked together in the New Testament. The way to the
reality behind the kerygma is barred in the gospels by the
kerygma itself. In his little book, *Jesus* (1,26), Rudolf Bultmann said: 'I am . . . of the opinion that we can know
practically nothing more about the life . . . of Jesus, because
the Christian sources were not interested in it, because they
are moreover very fragmentary and overgrown with legends
and because we do not have any other sources at our disposal.'
Bultmann was not unhappy with this situation, nor was Karl
Barth. Bultmann after all maintained that faith was not
concerned with historical facts, but with the new 'understanding of self' that comes about as a result of the encounter
with the kerygma of the cross and the resurrection, and
whatever continuity there is or is not between the kerygma
and the historical reality behind the gospels is of no importance. It would take us no farther if we could say with certainty or with great probability that Jesus really said or did
this or that. Faith, then, has nothing to do with the historical
Jesus. It has only to do with the kerygmatic, eschatological
Christ. We find an analogous situation in the writings of
Karl Barth. Supposing that historical research were to
succeed in saying something or other about the historical
Jesus—what then? It cannot tell us who he is. Only the
testimony of holy Scripture can tell us that—he is the Word
of God, he is the Lord and so on. We should not seek behind

the text, but be guided in faith by the text. The quest for the historical Jesus is of no importance to faith.

But Bultmann's followers have once more taken up the quest in the New Testament for the historical Jesus. This is not, however, a return to the research into the life of Jesus of the nineteenth century. Ernst Käsemann, Günther Born-kamm and the rest take as their point of departure the fact that the gospels have a kerygmatic character and that a description of the life of Jesus is beyond our reach. Yet the question of the continuity between the historical reality of Jesus of Nazareth and the ancient Christian kerygma must still be asked. 'The quest for the historical Jesus is legitimate as the quest for the continuity of the gospel in the discon-tinuity of the age and in the variety of the kerygma.' The variety of the kerygma . . . The New Testament used various models in its testimony concerning the Lord and these cannot be brought together into a single model. But all these models were, so to speak, suggested by Jesus himself. We cannot write a biography, we can differ about the authenticity of many words and we cannot say whether some of the accounts go back to real events or not, but we do know who Jesus was. The Norwegian theologian, N. A. Dahl expressed this in the following way—the tradition concerning Jesus may, in its entirety, be community theology, but it is at the same time, in its entirety, a reflex of Jesus. Paul Tillich's Christology (*Systematic Theology II*) appeared in 1957, so that he could not, by that time, have assimilated the work of the new research. He does, however, use a happy formula, saying that there must be an *analogia imaginis*—an analogy between the image of Jesus that is handed down to us in the gospels and Jesus himself. We have, then, no more than models, facets or 'bliks' (to use Paul van Buren's word), but it is in these images, etc., that God addresses us and calls us to faith.

Nothing of the new research is to be found in Bonhoeffer, Bultmann or Tillich—that would in any case be chrono-logically impossible. In America, Paul van Buren and Carl Michalson especially have taken the work of Ernst Käsemann and the others into account. Van Buren, in describing Jesus as a man who lived his life in remarkable freedom, thus continues the work of this school. In this connection, however, it should be noted that van Buren, writing in this way about Jesus, does not provide a complete Christology. A great deal more than this has to be said in any modern Christology. Jesus's freedom, which spread to his disciples and which spreads to everyone who believes, is only one of the glimpses given to us by the kerygma and, even for van Buren, Jesus is more than 'a remarkably free man'.[1]

There is a strong reaction in the new theology against the classical Christology—opposition both to the realistic conception of the 'facts of salvation' and to the metaphysical Christology of the Council of Chalcedon.

As far as the first of these two reactions is concerned, the realistic conception of the facts of salvation amounts to incredible supranaturalism (Paul Tillich) or to clinging to a mythological view of the world (Rudolf Bultmann). We are confronted with a series of miracles which are said to have happened here and which do not happen anywhere else and we must simply believe that there is a hell below the earth and a heaven above it, that God the Son descended from his eternity to earth, that Mary was a virgin and that the grave was empty. But Tillich, Bultmann, Robinson, van Buren and all the other new theologians tell us now that we have no choice. We must interpret the events which have been handed down to us in the New Testament and which have been summarized in the Apostles' Creed in such a way that the supranaturalistic framework is removed from them. The account of the resurrection mentions the power of Jesus as the Christ in order to transfer the New Being beyond death to Jesus's own and to lead to Life's conquest of death (Tillich). Rudolf Bultmann, on the other hand, says that we have to demythologize the biblical accounts and interpret them existentially so that the real meaning and significance of what the first Christians expressed in the ideas and images that

[1]P. van Buren, *The Secular Meaning of the Gospel*, London 1965, 121.

were given with their mythological view of the world are brought to light. In the case of the biblical story of the resurrection, we find the mythological expression of the new understanding that the believers who had taken the cross on themselves had of themselves. As with the resurrection, so with the other facts of salvation. If we ask why this has to be done and why we cannot simply cling to the belief of the Fathers, the new theologians reply that it is because the traditional realistic conception of the facts of salvation, which is not prescribed for us by the New Testament, simply means that the Christian faith is no longer credible. But Robinson was, of course, right when he said that we have become poorer if we no longer hear the singing of the angels at Christmas and no longer see the star that led the wise men from the East and if we know that it was legendary angels who sang then and a legendary star that led the wise men and that the whole story was a legend calling for interpretation.

But all this means that more attention is given to the man Jesus of Nazareth now than in the past. Although the Council of Chalcedon declared that God the Son became truly man, what was of real interest to faith was that he was God, God himself. The fact that he was also man was a lesser truth. Now, however, the first thing that is said is that he was truly man, similar to all men and quite different. He is different because of his freedom (Paul van Buren), because he is unconditionally there for others (Dietrich Bonhoeffer) and because he has conquered the self-estrangement which at the same time estranges man from God (Paul Tillich). And it is in this way that he is the Word of God, or the Son of God, or the Christ or whatever symbols we may use—bearing in mind that, if we use these symbols, we must also interpret them.

What is the attitude of the new theologians towards the definitions of the Council of Chalcedon? Generally speaking, this is twofold. This is certainly the case with Paul Tillich and Paul van Buren, both of whom have been quite explicit about

their attitude towards these definitions. They both agree that
the Church, having made use of Greek philosophical concepts, could not say anything different from what she did say
in the year 451. No other concepts were, after all, available
to the Fathers of the Church! Tillich says: 'By intent and
design, it (that is, the christological dogma of Chalcedon)
was true to the genuine meaning of the Christian message.
It saved Christianity from a complete elimination of the
picture of Jesus as the Christ'[1] and van Buren is by and large
in agreement with him.

These two theologians, however, have more serious objections to the dogma. They object above all to the Greek
philosophical concepts which the Church Fathers used and
which we can no longer use. They had no choice, but we do.
Keeping to the 'intent and design' of the dogma, we must
speak about Jesus as the Christ in quite different concepts—
in historical, existential and relational concepts. Paul van
Buren has therefore developed a Christology with the help
of the concepts of 'call' and 'response'—Jesus was the one
who *de facto* and to the last consequence responded to the
voice which called him. This is, in van Buren's view, what
the New Testament meant when it called him the Son of God
and, in this connection, van Buren refers to the Old Testament and to the meaning which the term 'Son of God',
applied, for example, to the people of Israel, has there. Van
Buren emphasizes the true humanity of the man Jesus who
has told faith once and for all time what being a man is and
has thus given faith its historical perspective.

Tillich does something very similar. The being of Jesus as
the bearer of the New Being and as the one who resisted and
overcame self-estrangement cannot be adequately defined
with concepts such as those of the two natures. We have to
use relational and dynamic concepts. Tillich, however, avoids
the use of ethical concepts such as those of call and response
and uses ontological terms such as 'eternal God-man-unity'
and 'eternal God-Manhood'. These concepts point to the fact

[1] P. Tillich, *Systematic Theology II*, 163.

that Jesus, involved in the ambiguity of all life in history, nonetheless lived his life, in Tillich's view, in an unbroken though challenged community with God and in that unity of freedom and destiny which is one of the essential structures of human existence. We may, of course, question the suitability of such concepts as 'eternal God-man-unity', which strike us as so unhistorical, for the aim which Tillich set himself, but his Christology can only be understood in connection with his anthropology.

The tendency of the new theology is therefore clear. The confession that Jesus is the Christ, the Kyrios, the Son of God, is retained, but these are seen as symbols which have to be re-interpreted one by one. The *vere homo*, the true manhood of Jesus, is given an emphasis that it has so far never had in the history of the Church, even by Bonhoeffer and Robinson, and we are told in historical and existential concepts who Jesus is for faith. In a word, the new theology bids farewell, in its Christology too, to metaphysics.

Christ the Saviour

PAUL Tillich has written about Christ's 'work' in the last
chapter of his Christology (*Systematic Theology II*, pp. 191-208).
Here he explains what he understands by salvation, what
such words as Saviour, Mediator and Redeemer may mean,
how the Church has thought about reconciliation throughout
the centuries and what principles we ought to take as our
points of departure in the doctrine of reconciliation. Tillich
does not care for the traditional formulations and prefers to
speak about the 'healing' power which manifested itself in
Christ, which is manifest in the holy Spirit (the 'Spiritual
Presence') and which is the power of the New Being.

In the case of Bultmann, the reader should again refer to
the two essays in *Kerygma und Mythos I* and *II*. What Bultmann
has to say in *Kerygma and Myth* about whether a Christian
'understanding of self' is possible without Christ, is especially
important. He contends that faith and love—real life—are
only possible through an act of God, in other words, through
the event of Christ, and are beyond the reach of our own
possibilities. His essay, 'Das christologische Bekenntnis des
ökumenischen Rates', in *Glauben und Verstehen II*, Tübingen
1952, pp. 246-62, is also of importance in this connection.

Bonhoeffer's thoughts about soteriology (the doctrine of
sōtēria, salvation) are not systematically arranged in his
Letters and Papers. The most important theme in his soteriology
would seem to be that Christ liberates us from our 'religious'
possession by our own cares, desires, anxieties and so on and

that he enables us by his vocation to share in the 'messianic event' and to be there for others.

The new American theologians deal to a great extent with themes that they have taken from Bonhoeffer's *Letters and Papers*. For Paul van Buren, Christ is the one who has given us a new 'blik' and a new historical perspective (see especially *The Secular Meaning of the Gospel*, pp. 135-45). For Gibson Winter, he is the one who liberates us to historical responsibility and, for Carl Michalson, the one who overcomes 'historicity' and meaninglessness (see especially *The Rationality of Faith*, pp. 129-35). Harvey E. Cox has not written explicitly about Christology in *The Secular City*, but he describes the work of Christ as that of the exorcist who overcomes neurosis in man and in human society (see *The Secular City*, pp. 149-55).

Dorothee Sölle uses the classical concept of 'representation' here in a totally new setting, most emphatically dissociating herself from the whole complex of ideas traditionally associated with the word. The third part of her *Stellvertretung*, pp. 133-201, is especially important in this connection.

All the new theologians are opposed to the 'classical' doctrine of reconciliation as developed in the Middle Ages by Anselm of Canterbury and taken over by the Reformation. This classical interpretation of the work of Christ can be found, for example, in the Heidelberg Catechism, Sundays V-VI (alternatively IV-VI) and Dorothee Sölle criticizes it on pp. 93-6 of her book. In *Kerygma and Myth*, Rudolf Bultmann called the classical doctrine of reconciliation a mythological interpretation of the cross of Christ.

In Amsterdam in 1950, the basic formula of the World Council of Churches, in which Jesus Christ was called 'our God and Saviour', was laid down. Rudolf Bultmann made the following comment on this:

The statement that Jesus Christ must be recognized as the Saviour is so general that all the Churches are of course bound to agree with it. All the Churches are, after all, bound to endorse the statement in the Acts of the Apostles that 'there is salvation in no one else' (*Acts* 4:12). But it should in the first place be noted that all that is given with these words is a purely formal characteristic of Christ as the bringer of salvation and that it is left to each one of us to form his own ideas of the salvation that the *sōtēr*, the Saviour, has brought about . . . It should also be noted that the meaning of the word *Heiland* (Saviour) is extremely vague in German, with the result that most people cannot come to any definite ideas about it . . . I can imagine that the situation is better in French and English, because these languages reproduce the New Testament word *sōtēr* directly with *Sauveur* or Saviour. But I simply cannot understand how, for the German formulation of an ecumenical confession in the year 1950, a word could be chosen, the word *Heiland,* which has disappeared from German linguistic usage and has become a cipher.

What Bultmann says here is typical of the whole of the new theology in all its variations. The new theology is no less convinced than the traditional theology and no less convinced than Karl Barth that Jesus as the Christ has an absolutely unique significance for the Church and for Christian faith. As Paul Tillich has said, without the appearance of the New Being in Jesus as the Christ and without the continued effect of that New Being in the spiritual community, we should not succeed in escaping from existence in (self-)estrangement and our situation would be a seeking without finding. Rudolf Bultmann, on the other hand, has said that, without the event of Christ of the kerygma, there would be no way out of enslavement and of the treadmill of care, anxiety and sin into the freedom of faith, love and real being as men. Dietrich Bonhoeffer expressed it in this way: without Jesus, we would have to live without the experience of transcendence and we should not be able to transcend our own situation, but would have to remain the bondsmen of our religious illusions. In a word, the new theology is in agreement with Peter's statement that 'there is salvation in no one else' (*Acts* 4:12)—we have not to do with one of the prophets (*Mark* 8:28), with one of the heroes of the spirit or with one of Karl Jaspers's 'decisive' men, but with the Christ.

But if we say that Jesus Christ is the Saviour, we have still said nothing and we have nothing more to hold on to than a 'purely formal characteristic'. We have therefore still to interpret that word 'Saviour' and clarify its meaning. As with the great christological symbols, Christ, the Kyrios, the Son of God, the Son of Man and so on, so too with such words as Saviour and Redeemer. If they are not interpreted, all that we have is words, words, words—a fog of words in which nothing can be distinguished. And indeed, preaching the gospel is often no more than spreading a fog of words that are all too familiar but say nothing or at least nothing more to us.

We have therefore to interpret. And the interpretation of such words as salvation, Saviour, Redeemer and redemption is at the same time an interpretation of such themes—events? —as Jesus's crucifixion and resurrection. What does it mean to faith that Jesus was crucified and that the kerygma of the first community of Christians proclaimed his resurrection? As far as the crucifixion is concerned, Anselm of Canterbury provided an interpretation which held its ground for centuries. According to him, Christ's suffering and death on the cross were *satisfactio*, that is, satisfaction or, if need be, payment.

A simplified and abbreviated version of what Anselm said in his *Cur Deus homo* (*Why God became man*) is to be found in the Heidelberg Catechism. Briefly, it amounts to this. We men live in a situation of 'misery' because we have sinned, or rather, because we share in the sin of 'our first ancestors'. With our corrupt nature, we are 'quite incapable of any good and inclined to all evil'. This is the consequence of the 'prompting of the devil' and of our 'wilful disobedience'. God, 'in dreadful wrath', curses man (*Deut.* 27:26) and punishes him. Sin is, after all, a kind of *laesa majestas*, lese-majesty, because it is wilful disobedience! God therefore must punish us 'with the eternal punishment in body and soul'.

This is the situation in which Christ did his work for man's salvation. We have 'merited God's temporal and eternal punishment' and the question is whether there is any means by which we can escape this punishment. This is not easy, because God is not a Shylock but he demands that we should pay. (In the Latin text of the Catechism, the word used in this context is *satisfacere*, from which *satisfactio* is derived.) But we cannot pay, and our debt increases from day to day. The only one who can pay is God himself. Therefore God became man and we now have a Mediator 'who is at the same time both true God and true just man'. He can 'by virtue of his divinity, bear the burden of God's wrath in his humanity and gain for us justice and life'. Not only can he do this, but he has also done it. He humbled himself unto death 'since, because of God's justice and truth, our sins could not be paid for in any other way than by the death of the Son of God'. On the cross, Christ 'took on himself the curse which lay on me' (*Deut.* 21:23). Thus man's *miseria* is followed by his *liberatio*, his redemption. What he has done for us is credited to our account insofar as we are bound by sincere faith to this Mediator. In the Catechism, this account of our *liberatio*, redemption, is directly followed by the account of our *gratitudo*, our thankfulness. Terms like reconciliation through satisfaction, representative suffering, representation and accountability and phrases like 'for Christ's sake' or 'for the sake of the merits of Christ' belong to this context. Dorothee Sölle, however, notes in this connection that there is no question here of genuine, that is to say, of provisional and temporary representation, but that Christ has become, in this train of thought, our 'replacer'.

Anselm's doctrine of reconciliation was strictly logical. It certainly made it abundantly clear 'why God became man' and it placed Christology firmly within the framework of soteriology. It is also evident from Anselm's doctrine that the Church Fathers were not primarily concerned with a metaphysical theory, but with vindicating the claims of salvation itself in the christological conflict that raged during the early centuries of Christianity. These are no mean achievements. Yet his interpretation of the suffering and death of Christ is rejected by all the new theologians. If there is a complete consensus of opinion to be found anywhere among the new theologians, it is here.

Dorothee Sölle maintains that the 'representative' has become the 'replacer' in Anselm's interpretation, Bultmann calls it mythological and Tillich points to the antiquated legalistic terminology (which can, however, also be found in the New Testament!) and to Anselm's 'measuring' of the size of sin and punishment. But what the new theologians, together with many of the eighteenth- and nineteenth-century theologians, object to most of all is the idea that God must be reconciled and 'paid'. Reconciliation, they insist, takes place not between Christ and God, between the Son and the Father, but between God in Christ and men or between men mutually. The 'direction' of this event is the opposite to the direction indicated by Anselm—it does not lead from men, or from Christ as our representative, to God, but from God to men. We should not say that God is freed from the necessity—the necessity that is given with his justice —of having to impose temporal and eternal punishments on men; we should say that men are liberated and brought to themselves and to each other by Jesus's service or by God's act. At least, we should say this so long as we still wish to be able to speak meaningfully about God. The difference between Anselm's doctrine of reconciliation and that of the new theologians is, of course, not so absolute as I have indicated here—in Anselm and the Heidelberg Catechism, it was God himself who became man and what took place was the *liberatio hominis*, the liberation of man. Nonetheless, we have to abandon this 'mythological' interpretation of Christ's death on the cross. The cross of the Lord does remain one of the essential elements of theology and preaching, but it is different in our period of history from what it was in the situation of our ancestors and therefore it also 'says' something different.

Having indicated the new theologians' discontinuity with tradition, something must also be said about their continuity with the traditional teaching. Just as Anselm and the Heidelberg Catechism were concerned in this question with man's liberation or redemption, so too do the new theologians see the ultimate perspective of the cross as man's freedom. This is very clearly so in the case of Rudolf Bultmann, Paul van Buren and Dorothee Sölle—for them, freedom is the New Testament name for the identity that man is seeking. But it is also true of all the other new theologians. Although it is exaggerating slightly, it is possible to say that salvation and freedom are synonymous in the new theology. But if we say that it is a question of freedom, we have still said nothing— we have nothing more than a 'purely formal characteristic'. We have to interpret the word 'freedom' and say what it means.

It remains formal when we ascertain that two aspects can be distinguished in freedom—freedom is freedom *from* and freedom *to*. Bultmann, who examined meticulously what was meant by freedom in the New Testament, has said that freedom is freedom from the Law, freedom from death, freedom from sin and freedom from the world, in the sense in which John used the word *kosmos* in, for example, John 1:10: 'The world knew him not'. In all this, Bultmann went on, freedom is also freedom from the past and from the desire to have an overall view of our own life and to possess it and to find in it the certainty that always eludes us. Freedom is also freedom to live in faith and love and thus to obey the Law of God which man recognizes as the law of his own being. Bultmann described this freedom with the word *Entweltlichung*, by which he meant that the man who is freed is no longer the property of the world: 'The world has been crucified to me, and I to the world' (*Gal.* 6:14). This 'freedom from the world' does not mean that man withdraws himself from the world—it must be conceived dialectically. We are in the world, but in such a way that we know Christ, the *Logos*, the Word of God and are not the property of the world. This freedom has nothing to do with arbitrary choice—it can resist momentary inspiration. Here, Bonhoeffer is in full agreement with Bultmann: 'Only through discipline may a man learn to be free' was his comment in his 'Stations on the Road to Freedom'.[1]

We must define this freedom a little more precisely. Paul van Buren can help us here. The freedom that is given to us by Jesus is, he says, the freedom that he himself lived. This freedom cannot really be described, but its *imago*, its image, is before us in Jesus, in the 'bliks' that we find of him in the gospels. Jesus is the one who has defined this freedom once and for all time. He was free from himself, free from self-preservation, free from the anxiety that his life would be a 'failure', free from the sacred tradition and from the letter that kills (one might even use an extreme formula and say that he was free from 'God'), free from all the expectations which men associated with his appearance and from the status which men wished to give him (see *John* 6:15), free from care for the future and from anxiety about the possible consequences (see *Matt.* 6:25-33) and so on. And in this freedom from, he was—and here van Buren goes back to Bonhoeffer—free for the people whom he met on his way, free to listen and to reply and free to liberate. This freedom was an 'unmasking' of and an attack on the old world which crucified him. The cross was the victory—not the defeat—of his freedom and the kerygma of the resurrection was the confirmation of this victory. Man's liberation consists in this freedom being transferred to others and their henceforth living this freedom imperfectly, faultily and always returning to the old world in their recognition of Jesus as the Redeemer. Bultmann would undoubtedly agree that this is more or less what he meant by *Entweltlichung*, being set free from the old world. Van Buren, however, expresses it all rather more clearly, and in more concrete terms.

[1] D. Bonhoeffer, *Letters and Papers from Prison*, 202.

It is possible to say that Jesus emerges, in Paul van Buren's book, as the exorcist. It is Jesus who liberates us from our lack of freedom and from our 'possession' by, for example self-preservation, anxiety about the possible consequences and fear of 'what people will say'. This theme, which can only be read between the lines in Paul van Buren, is explicit in Harvey E. Cox's *The Secular City*. Cox takes into account not only Freud, but also Marx, not only the neuroses of the individual, but also the collective neuroses of human society in the conviction that full health cannot be attained unless 'wholeness' is restored to the entire community of men. What Jesus did in his own times and in his own Jewish environment was to liberate men from their projections and from their compulsive 'behaviour patterns' (in other words, from their religion) so that they could be themselves in an authentic human existence. The situation in the twentieth century is different from that at the beginning of our era and the taboos and the behaviour patterns which civilization imposes on man and which automatically estrange him from himself are no longer the same, but the activity of the Redeemer which is carried on by his Church can still be described as 'social exorcism'. There is, however, in this line of thought, the implication that it is only in collaboration with the social sciences that theology can tell us in the concrete 'who Christ really is for us today' (Bonhoeffer). Certainly, he is the exorcist, but what does that mean in our present situation? Harvey E. Cox has made a number of reconnaissances into this virgin territory in his book.

The two themes that Cox has taken from Bonhoeffer are those of man's liberation from 'religion', which he presents above all as a system of behaviour patterns, and of 'maturity'. The same themes are to be found too in Gibson Winter and Carl Michalson, who also acknowledge their debt to Bonhoeffer here. I shall not consider here how these themes are related to these authors' views of the history of the Western world and of secularization. I must simply place on record that this constitutes a first attempt to demolish the Church in her traditional, authoritarian form, the Church which lays down what we have to believe and what we must do and the Church which at the same time provides men with their 'religious' security. That Church is one of the powers from which Christ liberated us. He accepts man's integral autonomy, the autonomy that he brought into the world himself. Freedom is freedom from the Law, from death, sin, the world, the past and so on, but it is also freedom from the Church in the sense of freedom to decide for ourselves and to be personally responsible. In the words of Gibson Winter, 'the days of the Establishment are past'. As Bonhoeffer said, Christ calls us, not to a new religion, but to life.

The only new theologian in whose work the notion of freedom in soteriology plays a relatively small part is Paul Tillich. As we have already seen, the fundamental category in his *Systematic Theology* is the New Being. This New Being became a historical reality in Jesus and Jesus gives the New Being to those who believe in his name. In his elaboration of this idea, Tillich had a pronounced preference for the word 'reunion'—man's New Being consists in his reunion with himself, with God, the ground of all being, and with the people around him. Thus the New Being is the 'healing' reality (Tillich alludes to the connection between the English word 'salvation' and the Latin *salvus*, healed) and thus it can be said of the Christ that he is the Saviour, the one who heals man and the world. 'Healing means reuniting that which is estranged, giving a centre to what is split, overcoming the split between God and man, man and his world, man and himself.'[1]

In a strict analogy with what we have already seen in the chapter on Revelation, Tillich also says here that the healing reality of God did not only appear in Jesus as the Christ. The healing power is active everywhere in history, preserving man in his self-estrangement from self-destruction. 'In some degree all men participate in the healing power of the New Being. Otherwise, they would have no being. The self-

[1] P. Tillich, *Systematic Theology II*, 192.

destructive consequences of estrangement would have destroyed them. But no men are totally healed, not even those
who have encountered the healing power as it appears in
Jesus as the Christ. Here the concept of salvation drives us to
the eschatological symbolism and its interpretation.'[1] The
history of salvation is not yet at an end, but we know the
future and we are on the way towards it.

There is no mention here of reconciling a God 'in dreadful
wrath' by the sacrifice of Christ, nor of any contrast in God
between his love and his justice. God himself is the reconciling, reuniting, healing Reality and it is God who takes on
himself, in the suffering of Christ, the consequence of our
guilt. He is not reconciled—he himself reconciles, shares in
the suffering of men and accepts and changes them. That he
is the ground of Being means that men live from the power
of his reconciliation, often unconsciously, and even more often
resisting it. But who are these men? What is their guilt,
their sin and their (self-)estrangement?

---

[1] *Op. cit.*, 193.

Man

BIBLIOGRAPHY

PAUL Tillich's anthropology is spread over the whole of his *Systematic Theology*—a result of his method of correlation. Part II, *Being and God* (*Systematic Theology I*, pp. 181-227) is, however, important in this connection, as it is here that Tillich describes man's essential being; and so is Part III, *Existence and the Christ* (*Systematic Theology II*, pp. 33-90), in which he describes how, and in which respect, man is estranged from his essential being without having lost it. In Tillich, the word existence is more or less synonymous with being man estranged from the essential being, with the 'fallen' man of traditional theology. What he has to say about existence is therefore a hamartiology, a doctrine of sin (Greek *hamartia*). Finally, Tillich describes life as a 'mixture' of essential and existential elements and discusses the inevitable 'ambiguity' of life in Part IV, *Life and the Spirit* (*Systematic Theology III*, pp. 11-113). In all these parts of the *Systematic Theology*, man appears as the one who is seeking— seeking for the courage to be, which enables him to accept his essential finitude and to live, for the New Being, which makes an end to his (self-)estrangement, for life without ambiguity which is the real life. The answer to man's seeking and asking is God, the New Being in Jesus as the Christ, the reality of the holy Spirit or, in Tillich's terminology, the 'Spiritual Presence'. Alexander J. McKelway gives a good summary of Tillich's study of man in *The Systematic Theology of Paul Tillich*, pp. 104-17, 146-55, 190-8.

The question which Rudolf Bultmann put to the New Testament, the question which arose as a result of demythologization as the *Existenzialinterpretation* of the New Testament and which has to be answered by theology is: what is man's new understanding of himself or of his existence that is given to him in the kerygma? Once again, Bultmann's most important article is his 'Neues Testament und Mythologie' in *Kerygma und Mythos I,* especially pp. 27-40. Several articles in the collection *Glauben und Verstehen* are also important in this connection. These are the articles written in 1940, 'Das Verständnis von Welt und Mensch im Neuen Testament und im Griechentum', *Glauben und Verstehen II,* pp. 59-78, and the essays 'Adam, wo bist du?', *Glauben und Verstehen II,* pp. 105-116, 'Der Mensch zwischen den Zeiten nach dem Neuen Testament', *Glauben und Verstehen III,* pp. 35-54 and 'Der Mensch und seine Welt nach dem Urteil der Bibel', *Glauben und Verstehen III,* pp. 151-65. A good survey of Bultmann's anthropology (although, strictly speaking there is no question of an anthropology here, any more than there is with Heidegger) is provided by Walter Schmithals in *Die Theologie Rudolf Bultmanns,* lectures 5 to 7.

There is very little to find in Bonhoeffer's *Letters and Papers* on anthropology. The most important is Bonhoeffer's conviction that a new, religionless type of man is emerging and that, partly because of this, words such as sin, conversion and so on must be given a new, religionless interpretation. The new American theologians have attempted to explain what the gospel means to this new type of man, men who are living after the death of God, 'secular' men. Generally speaking, they have dealt fairly schematically with anthropology and hamartiology. In *The Rationality of Faith,* Carl Michalson describes sin as an anachronism, as a lagging behind in the progress of history and as traditionalism and this theme can also be read between the lines in Gibson Winter's and in Harvey E. Cox's books. Considerable emphasis is given to interdependence and communication as structures of man's being, to which Dorothee Sölle has added the theme of 'reliance' on others (see Dorothee Sölle, *Stellvertretung*, pp. 21-72, especially pp. 64-72).

In traditional theology man had his place in the history of salvation, which extended from the creation to the last judgement. At the beginning of history was the creation. Man was there, made from dust, but in the image and likeness of God (*Gen.* 1:26) and, as the *Confessio Belgica* of 1561 expressed it, 'able to conform with his will in everything to the will of God', just, holy and good. Then came the fall— a historical event which took place in the distant past but which changed the human situation for all time. Man subjected himself to sin and thus to death and to God's curse. He lost all the gifts that he had received from God. All the light that was in him was changed into darkness and he became the darkness which John spoke about in his gospel (*John* 1:5). The sin which occasioned this change was generally defined in the older theology as (wilful) disobedience to God's commandment, thus favouring a moral conception of sin. This sin of 'our first ancestors', as described in Genesis 3, was continued in the whole of mankind. As distinct from Roman Catholic theology, the theology of the Reformation called this original sin the *corruptio totius naturae*, the corruption of the whole of nature (that is, of man's nature.) Through this, man became the slave of sin and lost for ever the ability and the freedom not to sin. Everything would have come to an end with sin and the death which followed it— and this is not unjust, because sin is always wilful disobedience and 'we willed it ourselves'—if God had not taken our guilt upon himself in his Son, the *Agnus Dei*, the 'Lamb of God sacrificed in innocence on the tree of the cross'. This brought about a new situation for those men whom God chose 'in his eternal and unchangeable counsel' and whom he 'draws and redeems', but not for those whom he leaves in their fallen and lost state, 'into which they threw themselves', as the *Confessio Belgica* says in article XVI. That is the twofold predestination to which Karl Barth, among others, objected so strongly.

There were therefore two groups of people—those who
believed and those who did not, those who were chosen and
those who were rejected, those who would enter the *Urbs Sion
aurea*, the golden city of heaven, and those who would find
eternal death in the outer darkness. Man's ultimate destiny
was, after all, not in this temporal and transient life, but
beyond it in heaven—or hell. It was thus still a 'Christian
dogma' for Pope Leo XIII that we would only truly live when
we had left this life on earth (the encyclical *Rerum Novarum*
of 1891).

The new theologians have, however, also abandoned the
traditional patterns of thought in anthropology. To begin
with, the realistic conception of heaven and hell has disappeared. These are themes which call for a symbolic interpretation in Tillich's view or for demythologization and
Existenzialinterpretation in Bultmann's view. For Bultmann, for
example, hell is the mythological representation of the transcendence of evil which again and again obtains power over
man. As with heaven and hell, so too with the great visions
of the Apocalypse, with the new Jerusalem which 'has no
need of sun or moon to shine upon it, for the glory of God is
its light' (*Apoc.* 21:23)—they are symbols arising from man's
mythological imagination and expressing his longing for a
life without 'ambiguity', for the 'eternal' life.

But the new theologians have gone even farther than this.
They have rejected not only the realistic conception of heaven
and hell, of the new Jerusalem and so on, but also the
'Christian dogma' of the true life after death which was given
its classical formulation in Pope Leo XIII's encyclical
Rerum Novarum. The true life, 'eternal' life, must not be
sought beyond this temporal, transient life on earth, but in
it and nowhere else. This was one of Bonhoeffer's considerations when he contrasted the Old Testament with 'religious'
Christianity and wrote about the profound this-worldliness
of the Christian faith. The American theologians Paul van
Buren and more especially Harvey E. Cox express themselves
even more clearly on this point. Cox uses the words 'prag-

matism' and 'profanity' to describe the pattern of the secular
city. Profanity refers to the fact that secular man leads his
life entirely within the sphere of this earth and to the fact
that every trace of the supraterrestrial reality which once
determined man's life has disappeared. Cox's view of the
Christian faith, however, does not lead him to try to replace
this entirely terrestrial sphere of life by a different sphere of
life. He insists that it would be a grave error to attempt to
desecularize modern man and to trick him out of his
'pragmatism' and his 'profanity' or to free him from them.
If we add to this the new theologians' total repudiation of the
dualism of the immortal soul or spirit and the transient body,
then it is quite clear that very little remains of one of the
traditional themes that dominated Christianity in the past—
that of the life after death.

Let us now move from the future and consider the 'past'.
The historical plan, in which the history of man began with
the *status integritatis* and the fall which put an end to this
state of rightness, no longer holds water. It has become
clear—it was in fact already clear to some people even in
the nineteenth century, but certain truths take a long time
before they are generally accepted—that the first chapters of
the book of Genesis do not refer to historical events in the
distant past, but vividly depict the constant elements of
man's existence and of human history. Adam is not a man
who lived in the dawn of history and who at one fatal moment
of time put out his hand to the Tree of Life. Adam (in
Hebrew *'ādhām*, man) of the first three chapters of Genesis is
the file on which my name is written. Like the *saeculum aureum*,
the golden age of the Romans, the *status integritatis* belongs
to the world of mythological imagination. In our present
situation, there is no reason at all for the Churches to reject
the theory of evolution as they did in the nineteenth century
and as some of them still do in the twentieth century.
In his preface to his *Systematic Theology III*, Tillich
acknowledges his debt of gratitude to the great achievements of Pierre Teilhard de Chardin in his description

of evolution, culminating in his book, *The Phenomenon of Man*.

Although so much has disappeared—man's origin as a separate act of God, the *status integritatis*, the historical fall, life after death either in heaven or in hell—sin remains. Anyone who wishes to speak about man cannot be silent about sin. Modern anthropology is not entirely, but it is to a very great extent, hamartiology. The illusions of the Enlightenment—although even Kant recognized the power of the 'radically evil'—and of the nineteenth century are behind us. There is therefore a clear continuity with tradition here. There is, however, an equally clear desire among the new theologians to replace the older legalistic and moral idea of sin (or sins) by a more adequate definition. 'If we were just nothing, I thought, we could just take the steam-tram to Katwijk as everybody does. But what about hell, which which would unlock its gates for me after this short life, then?' This is what the little boy in one of the stories in *Gesponnen suiker* by the Dutch writer Jan Wolkers thinks. In the experience of faith—it may, of course, have been different in theology!—sin was the collective name for a number of sins, transgressions of God's strict laws. To go to the seaside by the steam-tram on Sunday—that was sin. The point of departure for the new theology, however, is that the word 'sin' does not refer to definite actions, but to man's whole way of life. If there is, as Robinson maintains in his 'new morality', only one thing that is asked of us, love, then there is also only one sin, the failure to love. According to this criterion, the father in Jan Wolkers's story, who dawdled with his family along the roads to Katwijk and back, did not avoid sin!

Finally, it should be noted that one of the most important aspects of the new theological anthropology is the attempt made—more in some cases than in others (Bultmann, for example, makes very little attempt here)—to assimilate the data of psychology and the social sciences. It is the absence of these data which results in the classical anthropology of theologians and even in a book such as H. Berkhof's *De mens onderweg* making such an impression of unreality. Whether they like it or not, theologians must take into account not only the insights of Heidegger and Merleau-Ponty, but also those of Freud and Marx. The new theologians have already begun to do this and in particular they have paused to consider the significance for man of Marx's 'totality of social relationships'. They have not, of course, simply accepted Marxism and psycho-analysis uncritically, but neither have they rejected it outright, as theologians usually did in the past. In so doing, they have also thrown new light on the tragic element in sin, of which 'wilful disobedience' was an all too simple characterization.

In the new theology, it is Tillich who has done most work in the sphere of anthropology. The rest of this chapter will therefore be devoted mainly to him. In Part II of his *Systematic Theology*, he calls existentialism 'the good luck of Christian theology' and he has indeed incorporated many existentialist themes, from Heidegger's *Sein und Zeit I* especially, into his anthropology. Care, anxiety, humanity as a 'thrown' design and so on—these can all be discerned without difficulty in Tillich's arguments.

The concept of 'ultimate concern' is fundamental in Tillich's thought and if we are to understand his anthropology, we must understand what he means by this concept. Unlike animals, which are absorbed in the moment, man has a future and lives with many different 'concerns'. He is always concerned with one thing or another—with his bodily needs, with an examination, with his future and so on. But over and above all these 'concerns', man also lives with an 'ultimate concern'—that his life will be entirely real, that it will be the authentic life. For, however vaguely, everyone knows that he is estranged from authentic life—

> Sometimes I am suddenly aware of the only real sin—
> that I . . .
> have strayed far away from reality.
>
> M. Vasalis.

Authentic life—that is our ultimate concern. Although we may often forget it and although we may in fact often contradict it, we live constantly in the situation of Shakespeare's Hamlet—'to be or not to be'. This ultimate concern of mankind is differently defined in different religions and cultures. The Buddhist's ultimate reality, for example, is different from the Christians. The formal definition of ultimate concern has therefore to be amplified. At the beginning of his *Systematic Theology*, Tillich says that ultimate concern is the abstract translation of the great commandment, the *Sema' Yisrael*: 'Hear, O Israel: Yahweh is our God, Yahweh is one; and you shall love Yahweh your God with all your heart, and with all your soul, and with all your might' (*Deut.* 6:4-5; *Mark* 12:29). That is the Jewish and the Christian answer to the question, what is reality? We must also bear in mind that the second commandment, 'You shall love your neighbour as yourself' (*Mark* 12:31), the commandment which brings our neighbour within our horizon and, with our neighbour, the whole of human society, is equal to the first. Christian faith is the interior orientation towards this commandment, or rather, towards him who lived this commandment, Jesus as the Christ.

But we have not quite reached this point yet in our consideration of Tillich's anthropology. We are still considering his view of the structure of humanity which precedes sin and faith. He makes a distinction between man's essence and his existence—the essential structures of man's being and the existential estrangement which takes place within these structures.

The fundamental structure of man's being—Tillich is orientated here towards Heidegger's analysis of 'being in the world' in *Sein und Zeit I*—is the 'self-world-structure'. Man's being is a being in the world. Man and the world are dependent on each other. Man is nothing without his world and the world is not there as a structured whole without man. That man is in the world does not mean, however, that he is merged into the world. Thinking and acting, planning his

life, he transcends everything that he encounters in the
world. He *has* his world. In this way, self and the world are
mutually dependent on each other—they are 'interdepen-
dent'. As Tillich says in Part I of his great work, 'The self
without a world is empty; the world without a self is dead.'[1]
The subject-object structure of thought is one of the modes of
this fundamental self-world-structure.

Further analysis of this polarity of the self and its world
reveals three different polarities, namely:

1. 'individuality'—'universality' or
   'individualization'—'participation',
2. 'dynamics'—'form',
3. 'freedom'—'destiny'.

It will be clear that these elements correspond with the
self-world-structure—just as no self is possible without (its)
world, so too is no individualization possible without participation in the life of others and in history, and no freedom
without destiny. The word 'destiny' was, with Tillich's
consent, translated in the German version of the *Systematic
Theology* as *Schicksal*. But *Schicksal* has a much more fatalistic
sound than the English word 'destiny', which is related in
meaning to destination. (It was used more or less in this sense
by Reinhold Niebuhr in his book *The Nature and Destiny of
Man*.) It contains an element of the future, not to say an
eschatological aspect, which seems to be lacking in the
German word *Schicksal*. Be that as it may, there is no really
adequate translation of the word destiny, in the sense in
which Tillich uses it, either in German or in Dutch. What,
then, does Tillich mean by 'destiny'? I, man, experience
freedom in my reflection, in my decisions and in my responsibility. I can think or act differently; things would also have
been different. Freedom, however, has its frontiers—the
violence of the facts cuts across my reflection and disregards
my decisions. There is, then, not only freedom, but also
destiny. They are not opposites, but correlated. 'Destiny is
not a strange power which determines what shall happen to

[1]P. Tillich, *Systematic Theology I*, 189.

me. It is myself as given, formed by nature, history and myself.'[1] One of the consequences of this structure of man's being is that it would not be right to define sin simply as 'wilful disobedience'. An element of destiny, of not being able to act differently, of tragedy is contained in sin too. All the same, I am responsible.

One further aspect must be added to Tillich's picture of man's being. Man is finite. In Heidegger's words, being in the world is being to death. Man shares in being and in non-being, he lives and he dies, and he knows this. Sooner or later, and indeed again and again, he experiences the 'shock of non-being' which makes him, confronted as he is with the nothing, ask about Being. The human situation— and here Heidegger's analysis of man is once again discernible—is that of anxiety. Tillich himself says that anxiety is present as soon as the finite self is conscious of its finitude and notes in this connection that this anxiety is part of the essence of man's being and should not be regarded as a consequence of sin. If Christ was truly man, then he also shared in man's anxiety. 'The biblical record points to the profound anxiety of having to die in him who was called the Christ.'[2]

This, then, is Tillich's view of man before there is any question of sin—finite, anxious and in a freedom that is limited by destiny, he plans his world and himself within his world and he asks about the Being that will give him the courage to be.

But that is not the whole story. Man is also fallen and there is sin, or estrangement, or—in the distinctive terminology which Tillich consistently uses, existence. The use of the word existence with this meaning is new. The word estrangement, on the other hand, has a long history in hamartiology. Augustine, for example, spoke about man's *alienatio* and the *Confessio Gallica* (art. IX) says that man, through his own fault, lost the grace that God had given him 'and thus alienated himself from God'. Tillich was not, however, thinking in the first place of Augustine and the *Confessio*

[1] *Op. cit.*, 204.
[2] *Op. cit.*, 3.

Gallica when he introduced the word estrangement, but of Hegel and Marx. The latter especially used the word estrangement or alienation to describe the human situation in the world of the nineteenth century. Tillich did not, moreover, aim to abandon the word sin and to replace it by words such as existence and estrangement. But the word sin does point more clearly than any other single word to the aspect of man's own act and fault in the situation in which man is estranged from authentic life, his ultimate concern.

In Tillich's theology, there is no question of a historical fall, a sin committed once in the distant past, and he consequently prefers to avoid the term original sin. He does, however, speak about a 'transition' from essence to existence and here we are confronted in Tillich's thought with a demythologization of the historical fall which ceases half-way. This transition cannot be situated in history because it is the condition of what we experience in history. It is a transition which could and, in a certain sense, had to take place because man is finite, anxious freedom. Finally, to describe this transition, Tillich has availed himself of the profound analysis of Genesis 3 which Kierkegaard made in *The Concept of Anxiety*. There are two important considerations in connection with Tillich's 'transition'. The first is that it contains an aspect of guilt and an aspect of tragedy—both freedom and destiny are present in it. 'If the one or the other side is denied, the human situation becomes incomprehensible. Their unity is the great problem of the doctrine of man.'[1] Secondly, this transition does not mean that man has lost the essential structure of humanity (his 'nature'). The self-world-structure remains and the ontological elements remain and man is still finite, anxious freedom in the midst of overpowering facticity. But in these structures, man is estranged from God, from himself and from others. He is no longer who he 'was' and who he has to be. The human reality must be described in terms both of essence and of existence and this means in terms of an existen-

[1] P. Tillich, *Systematic Theology II*, 43.

tial deterioration of the essential structures of man's being.

Sin or estrangement is defined by Tillich as unbelief, a definition that he found in the *Confessio Augustana*. On closer examination, this unbelief is similar to 'un-love', the absence or lack of love. Tillich also describes sin or estrangement as concupiscence, a definition provided by the early Church and which Tillich further illuminates by Nietzsche's 'will to power' and Freud's 'libido'. Finally, estrangement is defined as 'hybris', the 'self-elevation' of man who makes himself the centre of his world. Estrangement defined in this way adds a new structure to humanity. It is a 'structure of destruction', which is not really a new structure alongside the already existing structures—the correlation of self and world, of freedom and destiny and so on—but something which has a destructive, breaking-down effect on these structures. Sin is the demolition of humanity. One of the most poignant sections in Tillich's *Systematic Theology* is the chapter in which, with the aid of psychology, sociology and modern literature, he shows how man's essential structures are affected and how he gets out of joint and destroys himself—he does not intend it, and yet it is his own fault.

All this does not simply happen. We know that it happens. We are aware of our estrangement. This life is not life! Just as man, in his anxiety, asks about the Being that gives him the courage to be, so too does he ask, in his estrangement, about the New Being in which his estrangement from God, from others and from himself is ended, in which unbelief and un-love, concupiscence and hybris no longer do their destructive work and in which man is once again entirely himself. Tillich's anthropology is followed in his *Systematic Theology* by his Christology, for Jesus as the Christ is, as we have already seen, the bearer of the New Being and the one who enables us to share in the New Being, who 'brings us home' from our (self-)estrangement. 'Therefore, if anyone is in Christ, he is a new creation' (2 *Cor.* 5:17)—for Tillich, this summarizes the whole of the gospel. Man has been given an answer to his question about a life without ambiguity.

The Church

BIBLIOGRAPHY

PAUL Tillich's ecclesiology (teaching about the *ekklēsia*, or Church) will be found in Part IV of his *Systematic Theology, Life and the Spirit*. As in the case of traditional dogmatics, his ecclesiology follows his teaching about the holy Spirit or, to use his own terminology, the 'Spiritual Presence' which enables men to share in the New Being in love and faith. The Spirit is the founder of the 'spiritual community' which is, for Tillich, not entirely identical with the Church or Churches. We may say that the Church is the spiritual community, but then we must at the same time say that the spiritual community is only imperfectly and fragmentarily realized in the Church. Chapter XXVII of *Systematic Theology III*, pp. 173-260, is especially important in this connection. Tillich has written about the relationship between the Church or Churches and the kingdom of God in Part V of *Systematic Theology, History and the Kingdom of God* (see *Systematic Theology III*, pp. 400-7 especially). The theme of the latent Church is discussed in *Systematic Theology III*, pp. 162-5, 193-4 and 402-7. This theme, however, goes back to a much earlier stage in Tillich's development. He 'discovered' it before 1933, while he was still in Germany, where he encountered authentic elements of the spiritual community in the German socialist movement.

Rudolf Bultmann has discussed the Church indirectly as the eschatological community which has been liberated from its state of having become the property of the world and now lives in freedom, in his essays on demythologization and *Existenzialinterpretation* in *Kerygma und Mythos I* and *II*. More important for an understanding of Bultmann's ecclesiology are several articles in the collection *Glauben und Verstehen*. The article which he wrote in 1929, 'Kirche und Lehre im Neuen Testament', published later in *Glauben und Verstehen I*, pp. 153-87, should be read and even more important is his later article, written in 1955, 'Die Wandlung des Selbstverständnisses der Kirche in der Geschichte des Urchristentums', *Glauben und Verstehen III*, pp. 131-41.

In Bonhoeffer's *Letters and Papers*, the Church is discussed, especially in his 'Outline for a Book' (pp. 178-181). The fundamental element in Bonhoeffer's ecclesiology is, of course, that the Church of the future, with her religionless interpretation of the Bible, will not be a 'religious' institution, but the community of men who take on themselves messianic suffering in the world. For Bonhoeffer, the symbol of the Church was the suffering servant of Yahweh in Isaiah 53.

Ecclesiology is the main theme in the new English and American theology. This is certainly so in the case of John A. T. Robinson, who concludes his book *Honest to God* with an outline of the consequences for the Church of the ideas contained in his theology (pp. 135-41). This outline is further elaborated in his later book, *The New Reformation?*, the last chapter of which is especially important. This chapter, 'Living in the Overlap' (pp. 79-100), deals with the older structures of the 'Establishment' and the new experiments. Gibson Winter's book, *The New Creation as Metropolis*, is devoted entirely to ecclesiology, that is, to the task of the Church in the modern world. On the jacket of the American edition, the book is described as 'a design for the Church's task in an urban world'. In *The Secular City*, Harvey E. Cox has written in great detail about the Church as God's avant-garde in the history of the world and about the Church's function of exorcism in modern society. Paul van Buren and Carl Michalson have less to say about the Church, but the reader will find references in the indices of their books.

Thinking about the Church in the new theology is formally marked by its combination of insight into the historical character of the Churches and criticism of the Church of the past (which is, to a great extent, the Church of to-day!). As Robinson has said, we are on the eve of a new reformation and, in the words of Gibson Winter, the days of the Establishment are numbered. The 'religious' institution is finished, Bonhoeffer proclaimed, and 'by the time you have grown up, the Church's form will have changed greatly'.[1] Hoekendijk maintains: 'It is futile to call upon these Churches—the Churches of the West, which have become 'class' Churches— to evangelize if we do not at the same time call upon them to overhaul their lives and to introduce drastic structural changes'. *Ecclesia semper reformanda*—the Church must always be reformed (not: always more reformed) and this is even more necessary in our own time than it was in the past. All the new theologians are convinced that the Church of the future will look very different from the Churches of the past, although it is not yet possible to say with any certainty how this Church will look.

We are to-day far more sharply aware than Christians in the past of the great distance between the *ekklēsia* of the New Testament and the Churches as they have developed in the history of Europe and of the great changes that have taken place in the Church's 'understanding of herself'. Although it is still possible to maintain that the Church of to-day is the same as the Church of the New Testament and of patristic times—*Ecclesia semper eadem,* 'the Church always remains the same'—it is at the same time necessary to say that the Church has also become different. To confine ourselves to the very recent past, which is at the same time still the future, the Roman Catholic Church of the period since the Second Vatican Council is a different Church from the Counter-Reformation Church, which survived more or less until 1960. Certainly it is the 'same' Church and there is an unmistakable continuity with the past—with tradition—

[1] D. Bonhoeffer, *Letters and Papers from Prison,* 172.

but her 'understanding of herself' has changed. Indeed, the historicity of the Church goes so far that we are bound to state quite simply that the Church, in the sense in which we speak about Church in the New Testament, does not occur. It is, of course, true that the New Testament does refer to the *ekklēsia*, often in the plural, and we have no other translation for this than Church or community. But there is no reference in the New Testament to a Church with her offices, her hierarchy, her 'clergy line', to use John A. T. Robinson's phrase, her Church order, her *Codex iuris canonici* or her jurisdiction. The New Testament does not speak of the Church as a power in human society or of the responsibilities that accompany this power. The New Testament has nothing to say about the unholy alliance with the existing relationships or about many other things. All that we find in the New Testament is a 'messianic synagogue', its members living in the last days in faith, hope and love and knowing themselves, 'with glad and generous hearts' (*Acts* 2:46), to be guided by the holy Spirit. It can be established that the later Churches developed from this beginning. Something of the logic of this development—a logic that is connected, among other things, with the continuance of the last days and with the fact that the end did not come, as well as with the fact that the structures of secular society were imitated—can be demonstrated. But it cannot be denied that the Church has become different, irrevocably different. Nor can it be denied that the existing structures of the Church cannot be justified by referring to the New Testament. Bultmann has, after all, shown, in the above-mentioned essays in *Glauben und Verstehen* and in his *Theologie des Neuen Testaments*, that the Church's 'understanding of herself' already changed during the New Testament period.

Things which pass unnoticed during periods of great stability and equilibrium are seen clearly when the structures of human society are rapidly changing. As a consequence, we are also far more acutely conscious to-day than Christians of earlier generations of the ease and, generally speaking,

the lack of reserve with which the Churches have identified
themselves in the past with the powers which had the
management of affairs in society. Throne and altar went side
by side. God, the Netherlands and the House of Orange were
in league with each other. The Church was allied to capital
and, in the United States, the Church went together with the
American way of life. Everywhere and at all times, Authority
—in this context, the word must be written with a capital
letter—could count on the Church. If any body ever undermined Authority, it was certainly never the Church! It was
not by chance, but rather symptomatic of the history of the
Church in Europe that even Luther, whose appearance
occasioned such a radical break in the continuity of European
history, called on the noblemen of the German nation to
fight against the 'rapacious' peasants!

It is therefore not only a question of changes in the
Church's 'understanding of herself' throughout the centuries,
but also a question of an almost dramatic contrast between
the *ekklēsia* of the New Testament and the Churches of European history. The *ekklēsia* was, as the eschatological community (R. Bultmann), the form of God's future in an old world
and therefore a revolutionary force, even if the *ekklēsia*, living,
as she was, in the last days, did not directly attack the structures of society. She was ahead of her time, the avant-garde of
humanity on the way to the kingdom—a theme that Harvey
E. Cox has taken up again in *The Secular City*. In European
history, however, the Churches became the great powers of
conservatism, the anachronistic *laudatores temporis acti* (and
anachronism is, at least in Carl Michalson's opinion, the
same as sin!), the accomplices of every *ancien régime*.
Generally speaking, this was so in the case of science. It was
often the case in the struggle for social justice. It was also the
case in France in the eighteenth century and in Prussia and
Russia in the nineteenth. In the twentieth century, we have
witnessed the attitude of the Churches, and especially of the
Roman Catholic Church, which has not yet been fully
explained, towards national socialism and fascism. How the

Churches have been able to (and have wanted to) play this part is one of the most disheartening puzzles of history.

The new theologians' critical attitude towards the Churches of the past, which are, it must be stressed by repetition, still to a very great extent the Churches of to-day, has not been prompted by social and historical considerations alone. It is also connected with what Paul Tillich called the 'Protestant principle' that every historical reality relies on grace for its 'justification', because every historical reality—and the Churches are no exception to this!—shares in the 'ambiguity' of all life and in the existential estrangement from Being. It is certainly true that the creative 'Spiritual Presence' is active in the Churches, making them a 'spiritual community', one, holy and catholic (cf. the Apostles' Creed), but it is also true that the ambiguity and estrangement are there as well. It is for this reason that the Churches especially must be subjected to that prophetic and Protestant criticism which is opposed to all 'self-elevation'—'whoever exalts himself will be humbled' (*Matt.* 23:12). The Church too can only exist *sola gratia*, by grace alone. The Churches are, after all, not what they are!

In outlining the image of the Church of the future, many of the new theologians take as their point of departure Bonhoeffer's idea that the most characteristic aspect of the Church, her first and foremost 'mark', is her being there for others. This was, for Bonhoeffer, the link between Christology and ecclesiology. Jesus was there entirely for others and he was not bound by the natural law of self-preservation, Spinoza's *suum esse conservare* which makes itself felt everywhere. The Church must also be there in this way, as a stranger in the midst of all those institutions which are intent on preserving themselves, on increasing their power and on becoming stronger and stronger. 'Whoever loses his life . . .' (*Matt.* 16:25). The Church of the future must therefore be one which is constantly losing herself for the world and constantly emerging, rising again new from the creative presence of the Spirit.

A distinction is made in traditional ecclesiology between the *ecclesia militans*, the militant Church, fighting her battle on earth and in history, and the *ecclesia triumphans*, the victorious Church in heaven and in the future. A great deal can be said, however, about the dialectical identity of the *ecclesia militans* and the *ecclesia triumphans*. Since the time of Constantine the Great, the *ecclesia militans* has, at least in principle, also been the ruling Church. Dorothee Sölle has commented bitterly on this ruling Church and its attitude towards the Jews in her book *Stellvertretung* and all the new theologians have turned their backs upon the social, cultural and political claims to power of the Church of the Constantinian and post-Constantinian era.

As Gibson Winter has said, the Church of the future will be the 'Servant-Church' which will be in the world without any claims to power, in the strange manner of the servant of Yahweh of Isaiah 53. Whatever consequences this may have for the structures of the Church, it certainly means a fundamental break with the age-old alliance with the Throne, Order, Authority, Capital and so on. What the Church will say and do can no longer be said in advance. She herself cannot tell this in advance. She can only take up her stand unexpectedly at the side of the poor, those without rights or power, those who have nothing to say and who have 'but to do or die'. She can take up her stand where she belongs. She can become a revolutionary element in society, no longer impressed by Order, Authority and Tradition, but obedient to the future. She can become untrustworthy—and worthy of belief. It is possible. But whether it will happen or not, we cannot say. There is, however, a vital conviction in the new theology that we are on the verge of a new era in the history of the Church, an era which contains new possibilities.

The point of departure in sketching out the Church of the future is that it is not a question of the Church in history, but of the world—or the *Oikoumenē* (see *Luke* 2:1)—and the kingdom, and that the Church is therefore not an end, but a means. This has been emphasized by Professor Hoekendijk

especially, although he is not the only theologian to have
stressed this point. In his essay, 'Kerk in perspectief', included
in the collection *De kerk binnenste buiten*, he has written:
'Ecclesiology can be only one single paragraph of Christology
(*messianic* action with the world) and a few sentences of
eschatology (messianic action with the *world*) and no more
than this. For the Church is only really Church insofar as she
allows herself to be entirely absorbed in and used in God's
action with the *oikoumenē*. That is why she cannot be other
than always "ecumenical", that is, concerned with the
oikoumenē, the whole world.' In his elaboration of this idea,
Hoekendijk makes clear that it is a question in history of the
šālôm, which Hoekendijk translates as the 'salvation of the
kingdom', brought to the world in the kerygma, the
koinonia and the *diākonia*, in the message, community and
service. 'In her existence, she (that is, the Church) will set
up the signs of the salvation of the kingdom: community,
justice, unity and so on. The Church cannot be more than a
sign. She points away from herself towards the kingdom and
allows herself to be used for and by the kingdom in the
oikoumenē. There is nothing that the Church can demand and
nothing that she can possess for herself . . . God has placed
her in a living relationship with the kingdom and the
oikoumenē. It is only *in actu,* in the carrying out of her apostolate, which means in communicating the gospel of the kingdom to the *oikoumenē,* that the Church exists.' To express it in
an extreme form, the Church is not, she is becoming,
happening wherever the kingdom gains form in the world
in *kerygma, koinonia* and *diākonia*.

This idea of the Church's threefold function in the world
recurs in Harvey E. Cox's book *The Secular City* in the chapter
in which he describes the Church as God's *avant-garde* in the
world. The way in which the service of the 'Servant-Church'
in the world is described by Gibson Winter, who regards
theological reflection as the Church's essential task, and by
Harvey E. Cox, who believes this task to be that of exorcism
and the making visible of the 'City of Man', will be found

briefly outlined in my chapter on the new American theology.

In the perspective of these ideas, the Church of the future will consist of small groups which will almost invisibly—as the salt of the earth—do their work in proclaiming the message, in community and in service, not alongside the structures of society, but within these structures. And it goes without saying that the 'clergy line', the division of the Church into those bearing office and the laity, will be broken through in this new situation. This, of course, is very much in accordance with Bonhoeffer's notes about the coming of age which is the consequence of centuries of growth and development. Both John A. T. Robinson and Gibson Winter have placed great emphasis on the fact that the Church of the future will be a Church of lay people and have pointed in this connection to the derivation of the word 'lay' via the Latin *laicus* and the Greek *laikos* from the New Testament *laos*, the people of God. The Church of the future will therefore be a Church without offices or, in any case, a Church in which the offices are given very little emphasis and office and authority are less closely connected with each other than in the past. The reader will therefore look in vain for a theology of office in Tillich, Bonhoeffer, and the other new theologians. Bultmann has contended that there was no antithesis between priests and laymen in the New Testament—although there were *episkopoi* ('overseers') in the early communities— and that an unhappy change took place in the Church's 'understanding of herself' when this antithesis came about at an early stage of the Church's history, making the Church into the 'institution of salvation' which, in essence, she was not. In one of the few comments on office and the hierarchy that can be found in the *Systematic Theology*, Paul Tillich has said: 'It (that is, the Church) must avoid the institutional profanation of the Spirit which took place in the early Catholic Church as a result of its replacement of *charisma* with office.'[1] Confronted with the dilemma of Bonhoeffer's being and act, de Lubac's institution and event, office and

[1] P. Tillich, *Systematic Theology III*, 125.

15

charisma, the new theologians unhesitatingly choose the second. The hierarchical structure of the Church, with its inevitable consequence of a 'clergy line', has no future at all in their train of thought. The whole edifice of the ecclesiastical hierarchy, including its ultimate, logical development—the form it acquired in the Roman Catholic Church at the First Vatican Council—has been undermined and must disappear. Is this simply a wish or its fulfilment in reality? Whatever it is, it cannot be denied that there is a consistent logic in this train of thought. As John A. T. Robinson has said, 'The old Reformation was compatible with the survival of clericalism, and indeed its reassertion in fresh forms . . . The new Reformation must see it go, if the whole Body of Christ is really to be released for its ministry to the world.'[1]

Gibson Winter has used the word *anamnēsis* and Harvey E. Cox has used the word 'exorcism' to define the task of the Church to-day. This is bound to have consequences as well for the place of preachers, ministers or priests in the Church and for their task and their training. An analysis of this task and of the special demands that it will make on the training of ministers lie, however, outside the scope of this book.

I have testified above to the relative character of the Church. Every form in which the Church appears is historical and relative. This form can always be different and sometimes it has to be different. Although it must always hold good that 'the powers of death (the "gates of Hades") shall not prevail against' the Church (*Matt.* 16:18), the forms and structures within which she performs her work in the world are less permanent and are not without 'ambiguity'. And if a Church presumes to be more than a historical form in which the Church appears, Tillich's Protestant principle is bound to be applied at once as a basis of criticism.

Tillich, in writing in the *Systematic Theology* about a latent, hidden Church outside the manifest Church (a distinction which is not the same as the traditional one between the invisible and the visible Church), and Dorothee Sölle, in the

[1] J. A. T. Robinson, *The New Reformation?*, London 1965, 57.

idea that she put forward in her speech at the Church Convention of 1965 of the Church outside the Church (*Kirche ausserhalb der Kirche*), have taken the notion of the Church's relativity even further.

Tillich, as we have seen, recognized the occurrence of genuine revelation outside the definitive revelation in Jesus as the Christ. In his view, there is a 'revelatory correlation' which is authentic and which must be recognized as authentic revelation both in the Old Testament and even outside the world of the Bible, in the most primitive religious experience. As we have also seen, he maintained that the healing reality of God not only appeared in Jesus as the Christ—'all men participate in the healing power of the New Being',[1] which preserves them from self-destruction. The logical consequence of this is that the 'spiritual community' is not only present wherever Jesus as the Christ is confessed and that there is therefore a latent Church outside the manifest Church which confesses Jesus as the Christ. This Church is latent, hidden—but not invisible. People who can see what there is to be seen are aware of the power of the New Being everywhere around them. Where is it, then? Tillich believes that it is present in the prophecy of the Old Testament and in the synagogue, in the ancient mystery religions, in Asiatic and European mysticism and in Islam. He even refers to artistic and political movements and, although he does not name these, he is undoubtedly thinking in this connection of (religious) socialism. Even communism would, in his opinion, not be able to exist if it contained no elements of the 'spiritual community'. It is possible—and not only possible!—that this latent Church represents the 'spiritual community' better than the Churches themselves. 'They may become critics of the Churches in the name of the spiritual community, and this is true even of such anti-religious and anti-Christian movements as world communism.'[2]

There is therefore great scope for open dialogue and real

[1] P. Tillich, *Systematic Theology II*, 193.
[2] P. Tillich, *Systematic Theology III*, 165.

tolerance, not only between the Churches themselves, but also between the Churches and the world. But there are limits to tolerance. Tillich not only said this—he also demonstrated it in his clear and positive rejection of national socialism in his book *Die sozialistische Entscheidung,* which appeared at a time when very few Germans distinguished the signs of the times—in 1932. His criterion was quite simply, is it possible to discern anything of the faith and love which constitute the 'spiritual community' in a political movement? In national socialism, this was not possible.

In conclusion, we may say that very little is left in the new theology of the security which the Church, the mother of the faithful, provided for her children in the past. On the contrary, men are called now to take up their historical responsibility themselves and to live together without protection in history, which is a secular, human matter. As God's avantgarde, they are called to live in an old world and to proclaim, with a strong faith and with an authentic love, the Name of God who has called us from darkness to his light.

Faith

BIBLIOGRAPHY

TILLICH's exposition of faith will be found especially in
Part IV of his *Systematic Theology, Life and the Spirit*
(*Systematic Theology III*, pp. 11-314). The most important
passages are on pp. 137-47 and pp. 231-58. Here, a new
interpretation is given to such words as conversion, justification and sanctification and Tillich shows what the New Being
brings about in the lives of men—more freedom, greater
'awareness', stronger solidarity and self-transcendence. He
also discusses faith in the little book *The Dynamics of Faith*.
In it, Tillich describes faith as 'ultimate concern'. He also
outlines the connection between faith and doubt, faith and
community and so on and rejects the traditional misconceptions of faith. Supplemented by data from the *Systematic
Theology*, this little book gives a good picture of what Tillich
understands by faith.

As far as Bultmann is concerned, what he says about (new)
being in faith on pp. 29-31 of his article 'The New Testament
and Mythology' in *Kerygma and Myth* is especially important.
More on the subject can be found in Bultmann's little book
Jesus Christ and Mythology, (London 1960), especially where
he deals with the antithesis between faith and the world-
view. The reader will find references in the index. Various
other articles are also of importance in this context—the
one written in 1931, 'Die Krisis des Glaubens', published
in *Glauben und Verstehen II*, pp. 1-19, the article published in
1948, 'Gnade und Freiheit' (*Glauben und Verstehen II*, pp.

149-61) and finally the article published in 1958, 'Das Befremdliche des christlichen Glaubens' (*Glauben und Verstehen III*, pp. 197-212).

Bonhoeffer's notes on the antithesis between faith and religion and on the 'this-worldliness' of the Christian faith are especially important. These will be found in his letters of 5 May 1944, 25 May 1944, 27 June 1944, 18 July 1944, 21 July 1944 and 30 April 1944 and in his 'Outline for a Book' in his *Letters and Papers from Prison*. It is clear from Bonhoeffer's speech in 1932, 'Dein Reich komme', which was later published in his *Gesammelte Schriften III*, Munich 1960, pp. 270-85, that the 'this-worldliness' of the Christian faith was an early theme in his thought.

In *Honest to God*, John A. T. Robinson has dealt with faith, especially in the chapters 'Worldly Holiness' and 'The New Morality'. More important, however, is what Robinson has to say, in *The New Reformation?* (pp. 38-46), about 'inductive' faith. This term, which he would have done better to avoid, refers to a faith which does not proceed from fixed 'truths', but which arises from man's situation in the world. In this discussion, the author elaborates Bonhoeffer's objection to the question 'What must I believe?'.

Paul van Buren has used Ian T. Ramsey's analysis of the language of faith in *Religious Language* to define faith firstly as 'discernment' and secondly as 'commitment'. As with Bultmann, the essential characteristic of faith for van Buren is that it is a life lived in freedom. The interested reader will easily find the most important passages dealing with faith in *The Secular Meaning of the Gospel* by consulting the index. Systematic discussions of faith will not be found in the writings of Carl Michalson, Gibson Winter and Harvey E. Cox, but these theologians do make it quite clear in their books that faith and 'politics' are indissolubly linked. Politics here have the broad significance of working for a truly human society, for *sedhāqāh* (justice) and *šālôm* (peace or salvation).

The new theologians are all opposed to two misconceptions

of the Christian faith, both of which have weighty consequences and to some extent determine the image of faith
both inside and outside the Churches.

Faith is often thought of as the acceptance on scriptural
or ecclesiastical authority of 'truths' which transcend our
thinking. 'It is in the Bible' or 'the Church teaches that . . .'
and so I have to believe it, even if I cannot see the rationality
of what I am bound to believe. There is a clear connection
between the conception of revelation and that of faith.
Whenever revelation is defined in the way outlined in the
previous chapters, this definition of faith is inevitable. It was
most clearly enunciated in the dogmatic constitution *Dei
Filius*, drawn up by the First Vatican Council in 1870.
Chapter 3 of this constitution dealt with faith and Chapter
4 with the relationship between faith and reason. At the
beginning of Chapter 3, the constitution said: 'Since man is
entirely dependent on God, his creator and his Lord . . . we
are bound in faith to show complete obedience in our thought
and our will to the God who reveals'. In this context, there
was also an explicit emphasis: 'We believe that everything
(the Latin text used the plural here) that has been revealed
by God is true and we believe that not because we have
perceived the truth of things with the light of reason, but on
the basis of God's authority.'

It is worth while considering the full implication of these
words. If this were the case, namely that we believe 'because
we have perceived the truth with the light of reason', there
would be a certain autonomy. But this autonomy is rejected
in the name of consistent heteronomy—we are bound to
believe because God has said it, which in fact comes down to
'because the Church, which is guided in all truth by the holy
Spirit, has said it'. It is the Church which determines the
credenda, what must be believed, and faith is obedient submission in our thinking (and our will) to this supreme
authority. Protestant theology was not, of course, able to put
it in this way, but, even in Protestantism, faith was generally
regarded as obedient submission in thought and will to God's

authority, which meant the authority of Scripture, which was infallibly true. We may take it that being unable to believe in this sense was one of the reasons (though not the only one!) why many people left the Church in the nineteenth century and did not return. This reason still holds good in the present century.

In addition to this first misconception of faith, there is also the second, metaphysical misconception, which led Marx to call religion the 'opium of the people' and which was given its classical formulation in the encyclical *Rerum Novarum*— we shall only truly live when we have departed from this life!—and in Hymn 181:3 in the hymn book of the Dutch Reformed Church:

> Look forward, my soul, to the other life
> which thou shalt inherit . . .

The basic misconception here is that we are not concerned in our lives with this life, but with the 'other' life which is to come. It is especially here that the Old Testament, which does not recognize the life after death, makes itself felt in our present thinking about Christian faith.

What is this idea of Christian faith then? The new theology as a whole has, so to speak, been existentializing faith. There is a clear connection in the new theology with existentialism —with Kierkegaard, to whom Bultmann especially is greatly indebted, and with Karl Jaspers and Martin Heidegger. There is also an equally clear connection with the Jewish faith in the sense of the Old Testament, as described by Martin Buber in *Zwei Glaubensweisen*.

As we have already seen, one of Bultmann's main reasons for demythologizing the New Testament was his desire to make clear what Christian faith was and what it was not: 'The purpose of demythologization is not to make faith acceptable to people of our own times by critically touching up tradition or biblical statements. It is to make clear to these people what Christian faith is and thus to confront them with the choice, the decision that this evokes, so that the "stumbling block" of the question of faith is made clear not only to people of our own times, but simply to people.' Believing in response to the kerygma is therefore depriving ourselves of all the security which we can obtain for ourselves or which we think that we can obtain for ourselves and taking on the risky venture of the unprotected life with God which is the only certainty. Faith is thus a choice of life which has to be made again and again, an overcoming of self which is not a victory, but grace—an event which embraces the whole of life and changes it and which may therefore be called existential. There is no question here of love also having to be added to faith, as was the case with the Roman Catholic theology of the First Vatican Council. Faith is simply identical with life lived in the freedom of love.

Tillich uses the word faith for the situation in which a man or a group of people is grasped by an 'ultimate concern'. This purely formal definition, which applies to all faith in all religions and civilizations, has to be amplified in the case of Christian faith. Here, faith is 'being grasped' by the New Being which appeared in Jesus as the Christ and which confronts us and speaks to us in the picture of him that we find in the New Testament. In this context, Tillich also makes use of the distinction in English between 'belief' and 'faith'. In faith, man is so grasped and affected by this New Being in which the self-estrangement of existence is overcome (there is, for this reason, not only a mystical element but also an element of ecstasy in faith!) that he knows—this is reality. Faith, however, is not only knowing that this is reality. It is also sharing in this reality which changes and renews the whole of life and puts an end to the estrangement of man from God, from his neighbour and from himself.

Faith, in the sense in which Tillich understands it (and Bultmann as well), is therefore not obedient submission in thought to the 'strange' authority of the Bible or the Church. The heteronomy of the traditional conception of faith is over and done with. On the other hand, however, there is no

question of autonomy either—man does not simply consult
with himself and with the finite reality. The situation of
faith is that of the theonomy which extends over the whole of
life. There could be no question of Christian faith without the
Bible and the kerygma, but faith is not faith in the Bible or
in the teaching of the Church. It is a way of life, life itself,
which can be more precisely defined with words like love,
patience, simplicity, gladness, trust, the courage to be and
so on. But is it then not necessary to believe in God's omnipotence, in the empty grave, in Mary's virginity and so on?
The answer to this question must be that the question itself,
put in this way, arises from that misconception of faith that
has been rejected by the whole of the new theology. I cannot
ask what I must believe, because faith is reduced, in the
question itself, to the acceptance of what Bultmann has called
a 'quantity of affirmations'. This is presumably also the
background to Bonhoeffer's opposition to Barth's positivism
of revelation, to his question, 'What must I believe?' and the
comment that he did not amplify, that this was a false
question, and to his criticism of Barth's theology and the
Confessing Church, which have both led to our sheltering
behind the 'faith of the Church' and not asking, in absolute
honesty, what we really believe ourselves.

John A. T. Robinson has taken this thinking a step farther
with his idea of 'inductive' faith. It is true that it would have
been better if he had not used the word 'inductive', as it does
seem to indicate that faith can be constructed from elements
of human experience without the Bible and the kerygma.
Robinson does not mean this, however. Faith lives from the
Word. What he means is that we must not ascertain deduc-
tively and in advance, on the basis of Scripture and tradition
or confession, where people who have encountered Christ
somewhere on their way must eventually end and what they
must eventually believe—the empty grave, the virgin Mary
and so on. If a beginning has somehow or other been made,
if people have, in one way or another, been grasped by the
story of the gospel, then it is a question of trust and not of

'predefinition'. There may be a creed and a confession of faith. This is in order. But we must not ask people to sign on the dotted line, even if only by getting them to recite the creed every week in church. After all, the Church is an 'accepting community', a community which has room for people and not a community which from time to time pronounces an anathema and excommunicates heretics!

The sphere of faith is life on this earth and worldly history, not the 'other' life and the *Urbs Sion aurea*. It is probably here that the distance between the new theology and the classical 'religious' interpretation of Christian faith is the greatest. In the speech that he made in 1932 on the second petition of the Our Father, Bonhoeffer opposed, with Nietzsche's Zarathustra, the *Hinterweltler* who still had a world behind this one to which they could withdraw if it became too much for them here, thus abandoning responsibility for what happened on earth: 'Only those who love the earth and God at the same time . . . can believe in the kingdom of God.' Bonhoeffer also said of Christ that he does not call men to a 'religious' flight from the world, but that he gives them back to the world. It is only a step from this speech to the question that he asked in his letter of 5 May 1944, 'Are not righteousness and the kingdom of God on earth the focus of everything?'[1] that is, of ,the ¦whole Bible.

In 1964, the American theologian, Amos Wilder, said in a very good essay on 'Art and Theological Meaning' (published in the collection *The New Orpheus. Essays toward a Christian Poetic*) that if we are to find grace, it must be found in this world and not somewhere overhead. The transcendent firmament of the reality overhead, he maintained, which provided a spiritual home for men until the eighteenth century, had collapsed. Many other quotations tending in the same direction could be added to those already given in this chapter.

In this situation, the theologian's task is to define the 'terrestrial' significance of Christian faith for the individual and for human society. He must, in other words, say what a

[1] D. Bonhoeffer, *Letters and Papers from Prison.*, 156.

'this-worldly' Christian life looks like. He could, for example, say, with Bonhoeffer, that the most essential aspect of Christian faith is being there for others and he could also add that our relationship with God is absorbed in this being there for others. It does sometimes look as though this was the case with Bonhoeffer, if we limit ourselves to a few extreme and one-sided formulas from Bonhoeffer's letters. In insisting that faith is simply being there for others, however, we can easily reduce it to the level of guileless, friendly, humanistic 'fellow humanity', which is even less relevant than the equally guileless Christian charity of the nineteenth century. The theologian could also say, with Bultmann and van Buren, that the most essential aspect of Christian faith is freedom— the freedom which Jesus lived and which was, according to van Buren, transferred from him to his disciples and has thus continued throughout the centuries. He could also combine the two and say that this freedom is the freedom to be there for others. But all these formulas—freedom, being there for others and so on—are abundantly formal and they bring human society as a social and political reality hardly at all, or at least not entirely, within our field of vision.

And yet Christian faith has to do not only with human beings living in a definite social and political configuration, but also with this configuration itself. In history, Christian faith is concerned not only with love which is extended to one's enemies as well (*Matt.* 5:43-4), but also with justice. Christian faith is not only devotion to one's neighbour who is lying stripped, beaten and half dead at the side of the road —it is also combatting the robbers who have done this to him (*Luke* 10:25-37). To put it very simply, Christian faith is also a social and political commitment to the world which is evoked by such symbols as the 'kingdom of God' and Harvey E. Cox's 'city of man'. Whoever says 'faith' at the same time says 'politics'—the struggle for the *Polis* and for a truly human society and against prejudices, resentment, ideologies, the 'will to power', the established positions of power, intimidation and so on. In the words of Phillippe Maury, 'Politics is the language of evangelism.' One of the greatest merits of the work of such theologians as Gibson Winter and Harvey E. Cox is the fact that they say once again, clearly and insistently, that faith is 'politics'. To say this may not be entirely new—Ernst Troeltsch's *Soziallehren der christlichen Kirchen und Gruppen* are as old as the Church herself and Karl Barth made it quite clear in the controversy about the German Church that the gospel has a political relevance—but it cannot be said often enough, especially at a time when the old world is passing rapidly away and men are urgently looking for the structures of a new human society. If the Churches, by default of appearance, take no part in this search, that would be one more reason for regarding the Christian faith as over and done with.

No wonder, then, that the Old Testament speaks to us now, in this new situation, with a new authority. This is especially true of the prophets. Words like *sedhāqāh* (justice) and *šālôm* (peace or salvation), which, for centuries, were understood in a purely religious and not in a political sense, have now been given new life. But nothing has in fact been done yet. All that has happened is that a few new words have been given to the already obscure and difficult vocabulary of faith. What is more, nothing will be done if we do not have the courage to say what these words demand of us in our new situation— we do need courage to do this and we may make mistakes, with unforeseeable consequences! But theology alone cannot say this. What the terrestrial, political significance of Christian faith is cannot be said in advance. It can only be said from case to case as the result of that theological reflection in which all the people of God—lay people—are involved. Faith on authority has given way to theonomous *anamnēsis*, which discerns the way of faith.

For, in all this, the new theologians are conscious of the fact that Luke, in the Acts of the Apostles, called faith the Way (*Acts* 18:25-6; 19:9, 23; 22:4; 24:14, 22). Believing is following a way which leads somewhere—to the kingdom, to peace and justice. As Bultmann has said with great emphasis, faith is not a world-view which enables us to survey the world and to answer all the questions that men can ask. It cannot, for example, answer the questions raised by theodicy—'how can everything that happens in the world be reconciled with God's love?' or 'how can God permit . . . ? ' Surrounded by all the puzzles of the world, the believer *knows* no more than the non-believer, but he knows the way and he has the courage not to know very many things. Unlike the discoverer in Gerrit Achterberg's Ichthyologie, he cannot consult the tablet with God. All that he possesses is the beginning of a map. He must set out with this on the way and 'the blank spaces on the map unfold themselves before his eyes'. He may encounter himself on the way, because

> The cartographer seeks a nib so fine
> that he can fill in our blanks and thus
> make us present with God, each one of us.
> G. Achterberg.

Our map is not yet as complete as that, however. On the contrary, 'we are once again being driven back to the beginning of our understanding. Reconciliation and redemption, regeneration and the holy Ghost, love of our enemies, cross and resurrection, life in Christ and Christian discipleship—all these things are so difficult and so remote that we hardly venture any more to speak of them. In the traditional words and acts we suspect that there may be something quite new and revolutionary, though we cannot as yet grasp or express it.'[1] This was Bonhoeffer's situation in 1944. Has much changed in the meantime? It is difficult to say, but there are, in any case, a few more lines on the map now than there were on the map as outlined in Bonhoeffer's *Letters and Papers*. Some of these lines will probably have to be erased, while others will remain—for the time being, at least, since theology is written in time, not in eternity.

---

[1] D. Bonhoeffer, *Letters and Papers from Prison*, 172.